RECORD BREAKERS

People and Places

For a free color catalog describing Gareth Stevens' list of high-quality books and multimedia programs, call 1-800-542-2595 (USA) or 1-800-461-9120 (Canada). Gareth Stevens Publishing's Fax: (414) 225-0377.
See our catalog, too, on the World Wide Web: http://gsinc.com

Library of Congress Cataloging-in-Publication Data

Grant, Neil.
    People and places / written by Neil Grant.
        p. cm. -- (Record breakers)
    Includes index.
    "First published in 1994 by Watts Books, London, England"--T.P. verso.
    ISBN 0-8368-1951-9 (lib. bdg.)
    1. Curiosities and wonders--Juvenile literature. I. Title. II. Series.
    AG243.G735 1997
    031.02--dc21   97-6169

First published in North America in 1997 by
Gareth Stevens Publishing
1555 North RiverCenter Drive, Suite 201
Milwaukee, Wisconsin 53212 USA

First published in 1994 by Watts Books, 96 Leonard Street, London, England, EC2A 4RH. Original © 1994 Orpheus Books Ltd. Illustrations by Simone Boni, Luigi Galante, Rosanna Rea (*The McRae Agency*), and Stephen Conlin. Picture acknowledgements: pages 40, 41, 42 Royal Geographic Society; page 45 Popperfoto Ltd. Created and produced by Nicholas Harris and Joanna Turner, Orpheus Books Ltd. Additional end matter © 1997 Gareth Stevens, Inc.

Printed in the United States of America

1 2 3 4 5 6 7 8 9 01 00 99 98 97

RECORD BREAKERS

People and Places

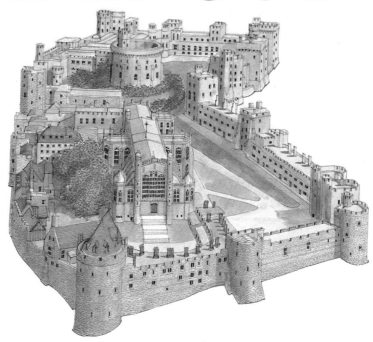

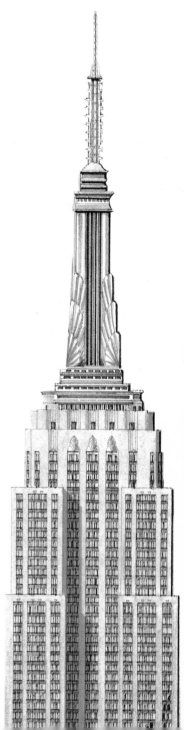

by Neil Grant

Gareth Stevens Publishing
MILWAUKEE

CONTENTS

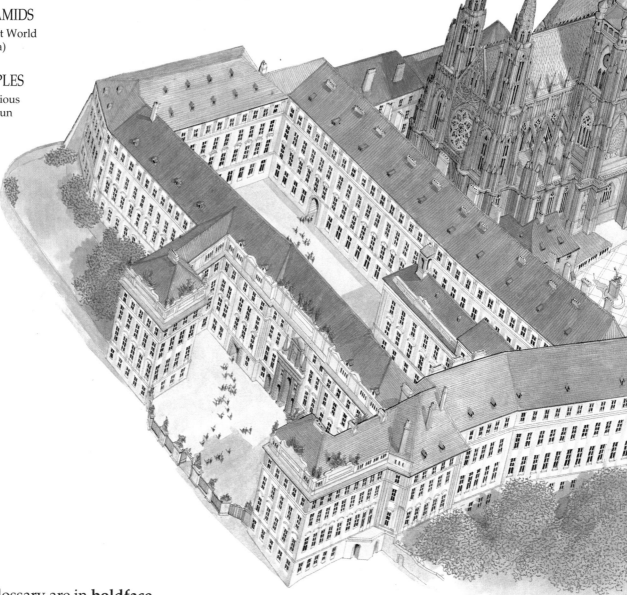

Words that appear in the glossary are in **boldface** type the first time they occur in the text.

INTRODUCTION

THE FIRST CITY, the oldest monarchy, the tallest tower, the longest bridge, the earliest paintings, the first person to sail around the world, to reach the North Pole, to climb Mount Everest, to walk in space — here are some of the record-breaking achievements of the human race from the Stone Age to the Space Age.

Sculptors who turn mountains into art galleries, kings whose tombs were ten times bigger than cathedrals, a poor young herdsman who came to rule half the world — discover how these amazing things happened by reading this book.

When Roald Amundsen reached the South Pole on his dog sled, he was the first person to make that incredible journey. To be the first was exactly his reason for doing it! But the millions of peasants who heaved stones up steep mountainsides to build the Great Wall of China did not know they were taking part in making the longest single structure in the world. Some of the achievements in this book were planned; some happened by chance. They all show the astonishing things humans can accomplish.

WORLD RECORD HOLDERS
FIRST AND FOREMOST FROM EVERY CONTINENT

1 Gateway Arch, St. Louis, Missouri **Tallest monument** 630 feet (192 meters)

2 Mount Rushmore, South Dakota **Largest sculpture**

3 CN Tower, Toronto, Canada **Tallest self-supporting structure** 1,814 feet (553 m)

4 Grand Central, New York City **Largest railroad station** 47 acres (19 hectares)

5 St. John the Divine, New York City **Largest cathedral (by volume)** 16,815,155 cubic feet (476,350 cu m)

6 Superdome, New Orleans, Louisiana **Largest indoor stadium** 13 acres (5.26 ha)

7 Cholula, Mexico (now built over by a church) **Largest pyramid** 45 acres (18 ha)

8 Mexico City, Mexico **Largest city** About 15,000,000 people

9 Morococha, Peru **Highest railroad line** 15,749 feet (4,800 m)+ above sea level

10 La Paz, Bolivia **Highest capital city** 11,910 feet (3,630 m) above sea level

11 Maracana Stadium, Rio de Janeiro, Brazil **Largest soccer stadium** 205,000 capacity

12 Ushuaia, Argentina **Southernmost town**

13 Greenland **Least densely populated country** 0.07 people per square mile (2.6 sq km)

14 Ny Ålesund, Svalbard **Northernmost village**

15 Rotterdam, Netherlands **Busiest port** 331 million tons (300 million metric tons)/year

16 Hradcany, Prague, Czechoslovakia **Largest ancient castle** 66 acres (26.7 hectares)

17 Heathrow Airport, London, UK **Most international traffic** 38,000,000 people/year

18 Ulm Cathedral, Germany **Tallest steeple** 528 feet (161 m)

19 Seville Cathedral, Spain **Largest cathedral (by area)** 381 feet (116 m) long; 249 feet (76 m) wide

20 Vatican City State, Italy **Smallest country** 0.17 sq miles (0.44 sq km)

21 Jericho, West Bank, Israel **Oldest city** Built about 10,000 years ago

22 Saqqara, Egypt **Oldest pyramid** Built in 2700 B.C.

23 Dinka people, Sudan **Tallest people** Average 6.9 feet (2.1 m) tall

24 Lake Volta, Ghana **Largest reservoir (by area)** 3,273 sq miles (8,480 sq km)

25 Bambuti people, Zaire **Shortest people** Average 4.6 feet (1.4 m) tall

26 Kenya, Africa **Highest birth rate** Average 54 births per 1,000 people

27 Russia **Largest country** 6,591,104 sq miles (17,075,400 sq km)

28 Forbidden City, Beijing, China **Largest palace** About 247 acres (1 sq km)

29 Seikan rail tunnel, Japan **Longest rail tunnel** 33.5 miles (54 km)

30 Tokyo-Yokohama, Japan **Largest urban agglomeration** 27,700,000 people

31 Amida Buddha, Ushiku City, Japan **Tallest statue** 394 feet (120 m)

32 Akashi-Kaikyo Bridge, Japan **Longest suspension bridge** 6,529 feet (1,990 m)

33 China **Largest population** 1,158,230,000 people

34 Shah Faisal, Islamabad, Pakistan **Largest mosque** 47 acres (19 ha)

35 Angkor, Cambodia **Largest temple complex** More than 97 sq miles (250 sq km)

36 Sultan's Palace, Brunei **Largest residential palace**

37 Petronas Twin Towers, Malaysia **Tallest office building** 1,482 feet (452 m)

38 Borobodur, Indonesia **Largest Buddhist temple** 161,460 sq feet (15,000 sq m)

39 Sydney Harbor Bridge, Australia **Widest long-span bridge** 161 feet (49 m) wide

40 Trans-Australia line/Nullarbor Plain **Longest straight rail track** 297 miles (478 km)

THE LARGEST CITIES

		approximate population
1	Mexico City, Mexico	15,000,000
2	Cairo, Egypt	14,000,000
3	Shanghai, China	12,800,000
4	Bombay, India	12,600,000
5	Tokyo, Japan	12,000,000
6	Calcutta, India	11,000,000
7	Beijing, China	10,900,000
8	São Paulo, Brazil	10,100,000
9	Seoul, South Korea	10,000,000
10	Paris, France	9,000,000

Figures are for the entire metropolitan area

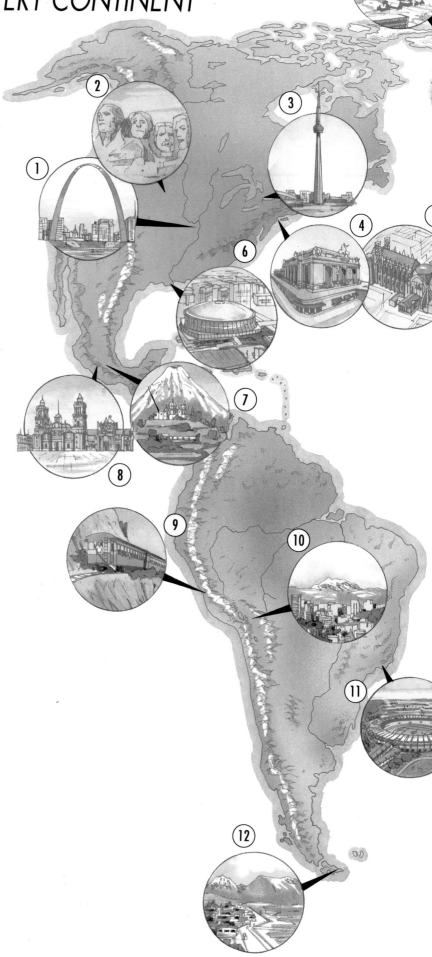

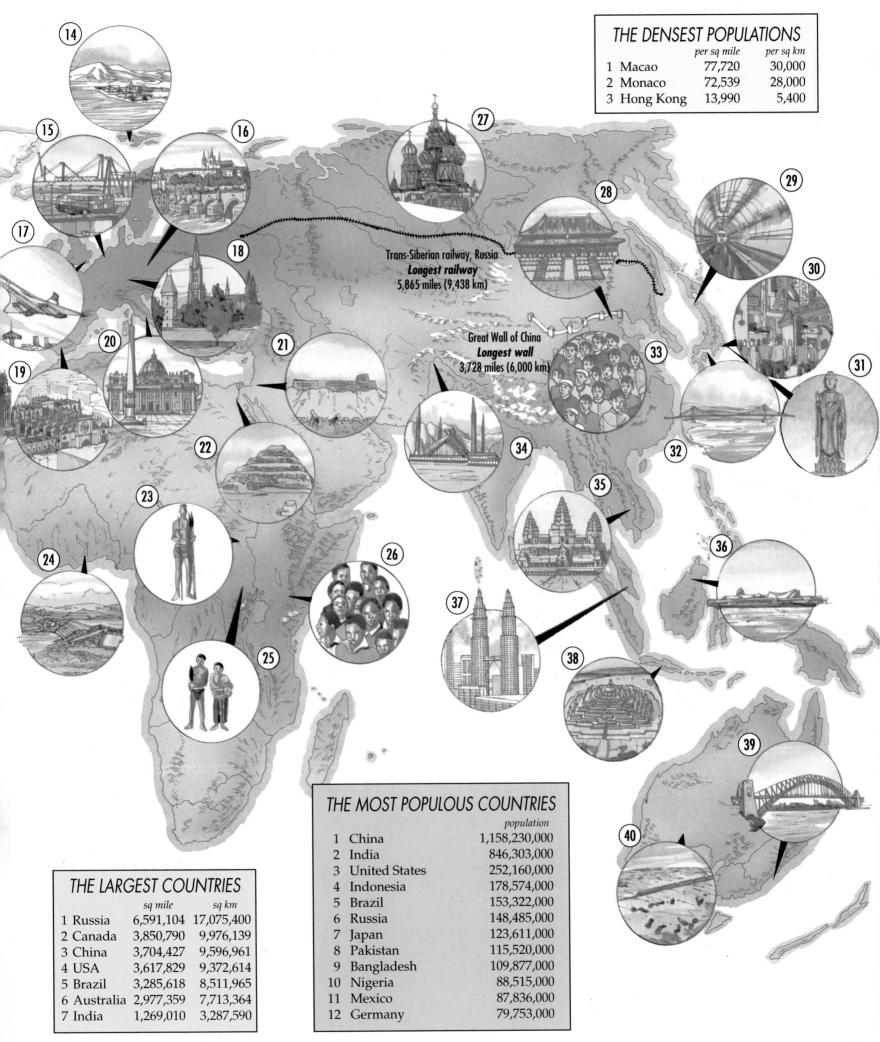

THE DENSEST POPULATIONS

		per sq mile	per sq km
1	Macao	77,720	30,000
2	Monaco	72,539	28,000
3	Hong Kong	13,990	5,400

Trans-Siberian railway, Russia
Longest railway
5,865 miles (9,438 km)

Great Wall of China
Longest wall
3,728 miles (6,000 km)

THE MOST POPULOUS COUNTRIES

		population
1	China	1,158,230,000
2	India	846,303,000
3	United States	252,160,000
4	Indonesia	178,574,000
5	Brazil	153,322,000
6	Russia	148,485,000
7	Japan	123,611,000
8	Pakistan	115,520,000
9	Bangladesh	109,877,000
10	Nigeria	88,515,000
11	Mexico	87,836,000
12	Germany	79,753,000

THE LARGEST COUNTRIES

		sq mile	sq km
1	Russia	6,591,104	17,075,400
2	Canada	3,850,790	9,976,139
3	China	3,704,427	9,596,961
4	USA	3,617,829	9,372,614
5	Brazil	3,285,618	8,511,965
6	Australia	2,977,359	7,713,364
7	India	1,269,010	3,287,590

THE FIRST ARTISTS
SCULPTURE AND PAINTING OF THE STONE AGE

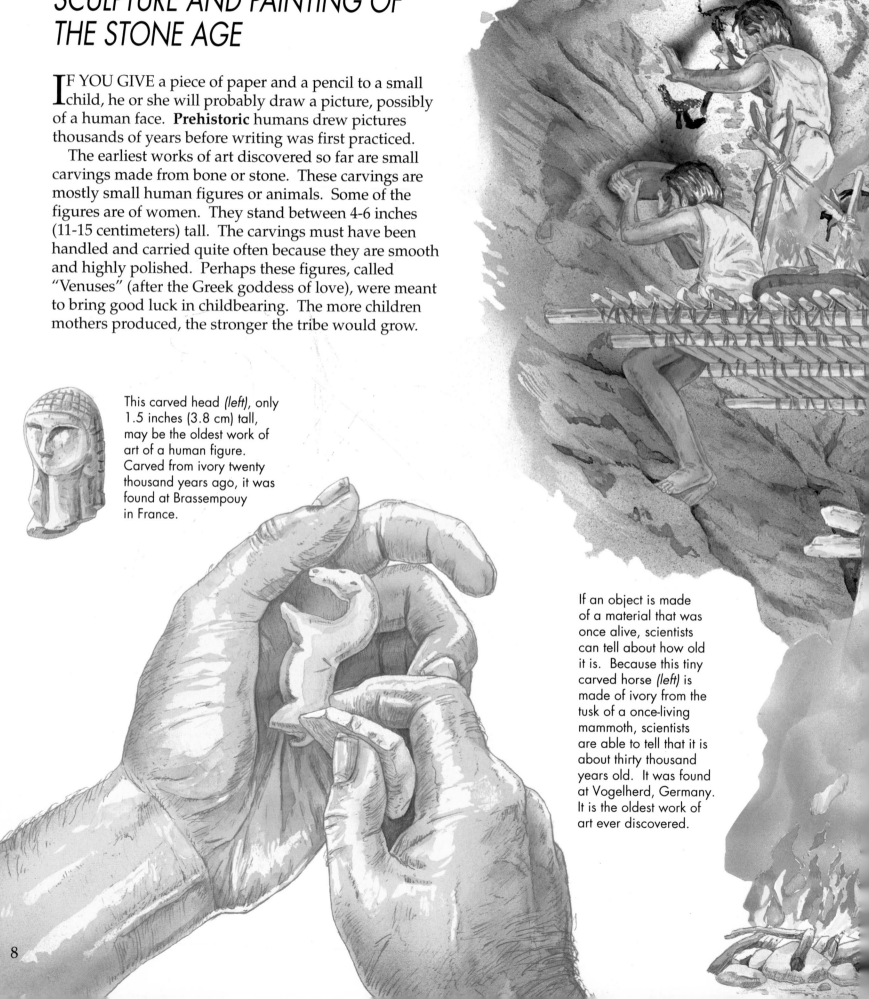

IF YOU GIVE a piece of paper and a pencil to a small child, he or she will probably draw a picture, possibly of a human face. **Prehistoric** humans drew pictures thousands of years before writing was first practiced.

The earliest works of art discovered so far are small carvings made from bone or stone. These carvings are mostly small human figures or animals. Some of the figures are of women. They stand between 4-6 inches (11-15 centimeters) tall. The carvings must have been handled and carried quite often because they are smooth and highly polished. Perhaps these figures, called "Venuses" (after the Greek goddess of love), were meant to bring good luck in childbearing. The more children mothers produced, the stronger the tribe would grow.

This carved head *(left)*, only 1.5 inches (3.8 cm) tall, may be the oldest work of art of a human figure. Carved from ivory twenty thousand years ago, it was found at Brassempouy in France.

If an object is made of a material that was once alive, scientists can tell about how old it is. Because this tiny carved horse *(left)* is made of ivory from the tusk of a once-living mammoth, scientists are able to tell that it is about thirty thousand years old. It was found at Vogelherd, Germany. It is the oldest work of art ever discovered.

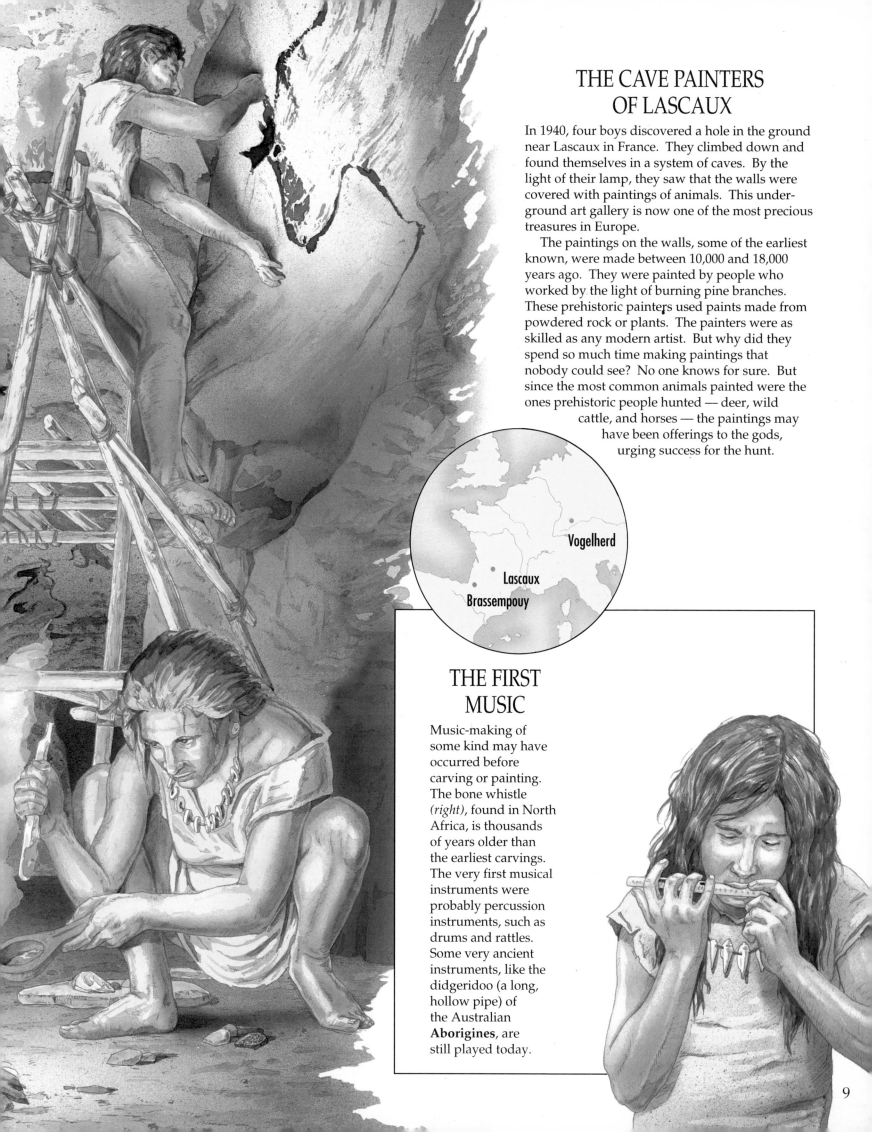

THE CAVE PAINTERS OF LASCAUX

In 1940, four boys discovered a hole in the ground near Lascaux in France. They climbed down and found themselves in a system of caves. By the light of their lamp, they saw that the walls were covered with paintings of animals. This underground art gallery is now one of the most precious treasures in Europe.

The paintings on the walls, some of the earliest known, were made between 10,000 and 18,000 years ago. They were painted by people who worked by the light of burning pine branches. These prehistoric painters used paints made from powdered rock or plants. The painters were as skilled as any modern artist. But why did they spend so much time making paintings that nobody could see? No one knows for sure. But since the most common animals painted were the ones prehistoric people hunted — deer, wild cattle, and horses — the paintings may have been offerings to the gods, urging success for the hunt.

Vogelherd

Lascaux

Brassempouy

THE FIRST MUSIC

Music-making of some kind may have occurred before carving or painting. The bone whistle *(right)*, found in North Africa, is thousands of years older than the earliest carvings. The very first musical instruments were probably percussion instruments, such as drums and rattles. Some very ancient instruments, like the didgeridoo (a long, hollow pipe) of the Australian **Aborigines**, are still played today.

9

THE WALLS OF JERICHO

The ancient city of Jericho is the oldest city ever discovered. There have been many cities of Jericho since ancient times, each rebuilt over the ruins of an earlier one. The people of the first Jericho learned how to cultivate wild wheat. They worked in the fields by day and kept safe from invasion in their houses behind walls at night. A watchman probably kept guard from a round, stone tower.

CRAFTSWORKERS OF CATAL HUYUK

Pictured is the ancient city of Catal Huyuk in Turkey. It is almost as old as the city of Jericho. Ladders linked the roof of one house with the roof of another. Once the ladders were taken away, entry to the houses was almost impossible. If attacked, Catal Huyuk was like a turtle, safely hidden inside of its shell.

Craftsworkers made ornaments and tools out of copper and a hard, glasslike mineral called **obsidian**. They made and decorated pottery. The walls of their houses were painted with hunting scenes.

TURKEY
Catal Huyuk

Jericho

EGYPT

PERSIAN GULF

Ancient cities were located in the "Fertile Crescent," good farmland stretching from Egypt up to southern Turkey and down to the Persian Gulf.

THE FIRST CITIES
TOWN LIFE 10,000 YEARS AGO

A T JERICHO, west of the Jordan River in Palestine, there is a spring that provides water for crops. That spring was there ten thousand years ago. It may be the reason why people first settled Jericho, the oldest-known city in the world.

The earliest humans were **nomads** who never lived in one place for long. They picked wild plants and hunted animals for food. When the food supply ran low in an area, people moved on. About twelve thousand years ago, humans discovered how to grow crops. They settled down and lived in just one place. They grew crops and raised animals.

Once people settled in villages, many changes took place. It was not necessary for everyone to spend all their time finding food. Farmers provided the food, and other people did various kinds of work. They became builders, craftsworkers, **merchants**, soldiers, teachers, priests, and more.

Town life first began in the Middle East, an area including the countries bordering the eastern end of the Mediterranean Sea. The very first villages were near the mountain slopes where wild cereals grew. Most of the villages were also near rivers — the Tigris, Euphrates, and Nile — where yearly floods resulted in rich, damp soil. Small hills, called *tell* in Arabic and *huyuk* in Turkish, mark the remains of ancient villages. Some villages grew quite large and had walls and towers. These were the first cities.

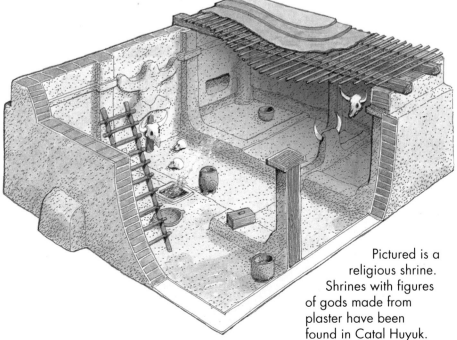

Pictured is a religious shrine. Shrines with figures of gods made from plaster have been found in Catal Huyuk.

THE FIRST WRITING
THE BEGINNING OF HISTORY

IMAGINE WHAT the world would be like if no one could read or write! There would be no way of sending messages, keeping records, or learning new facts except by word of mouth.

Writing is a way of recording language with symbols. In languages like English or Russian, these symbols are the letters of an alphabet. English has thousands of words, yet all the words can be written using just twenty-six letters. Making words out of letters is not the only way of writing. People used a written language long before an alphabet existed.

The development of writing as we know it was a long process that took thousands of years. It started where **civilization** began, in the ancient land of Mesopotamia (roughly, modern Iraq). The first items people recorded were lists, such as a list of the animals owned by a farmer. The symbols that stood for the animals were pictures. The symbol for *cow*, for example, was a picture of a cow's head. More words were created by putting two pictures together. For example, the picture for *woman* and the picture for *mountains*, written together, meant *foreign woman* ("woman from beyond the mountains").

WRITING WITH PICTURES

The first writing in picture symbols, or **pictograms**, that has been discovered so far comes from Uruk, a city of the Sumerians in Mesopotamia. The writing consists of records of goods and food supplies for a temple. The records were written with a pointed stick or reed on slabs of clay. The slabs *(above)* are in very good condition, although they were written 5,300 years ago.

Writing with a reed pen *(below)* in a wedgelike manner is called **cuneiform**.

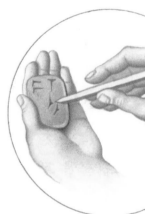

CHINESE WRITING

A Chinese legend says that writing was invented by an emperor who lived over four thousand years ago, after he had studied the footprints of birds and animals. The oldest Chinese writing found so far is on bones that were used to foretell the future. Priests wrote questions on a bone, then held it over a fire until the bone cracked. The places where the cracks crossed the writing were supposed to be answers from the gods.

The Chinese have never used an alphabet. Modern written language has developed from the earliest pictograms. These examples show how the symbols for *man* and *bird* have changed over about three thousand years.

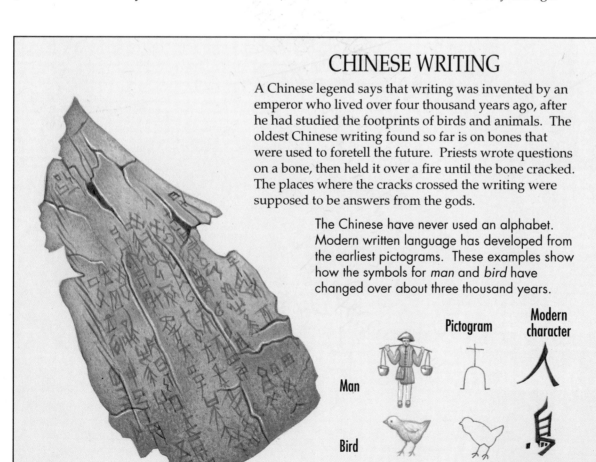

	Pictogram	Modern character
Man		
Bird		

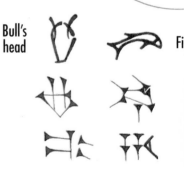

Bull's head   Fish

About 2900 B.C., the curves in Sumerian writing disappeared. They were replaced with straight lines that were easier to write with a reed pen cut to a point. This writing *(above)* is called cuneiform, meaning "wedgelike."

ANCIENT EGYPTIAN HIEROGLYPHS

A kind of picture-writing was invented in Egypt in about 3000 B.C. Symbols called hieroglyphs, meaning "holy writing," (*above, top*) were used. With **hieroglyphs**, it was possible to write poems, stories, and works on law or medicine. Writing hieroglyphs was, however, very slow. So Egyptians developed another, quicker form of writing, called hieratic *(above, bottom)*. The characters, or symbols, were based on hieroglyphs, but in a simpler form. They were not as beautiful, but much more practical.

The Egyptians were the first to use paper. They cut papyrus reed into strips and laid the strips side by side to make a square. A second layer was placed on top of the first, with the strips at right angles to the first layer. Papermakers then pressed the sheet flat and polished it smooth.

The first people to use an alphabet were the Canaanites, who lived in Palestine over three thousand years ago. Instead of learning hundreds of different word symbols, a person learned just twenty or thirty signs (letters) that stood for sounds. This made learning to read and write much easier. The modern Latin alphabet, used in the English language, has descended from the Canaanites.

Canaanite	Modern
⌔	A
⊓	B
∟	C
⋈	D
⚲	E
⍾	F
Ш	H
⌓	I
⊎	K
⌒	L
⌇	M
⌇	N
◉	O
⊑	P
8	Q
⌐	R
⌄	S
✕	T

A young Egyptian writes on a piece of pottery with a reed pen. Hieroglyphs were "painted" with a thin brush. Ink was made by mixing a powder with water.

THE GREATEST PYRAMIDS
MONUMENTS OF THE ANCIENT WORLD

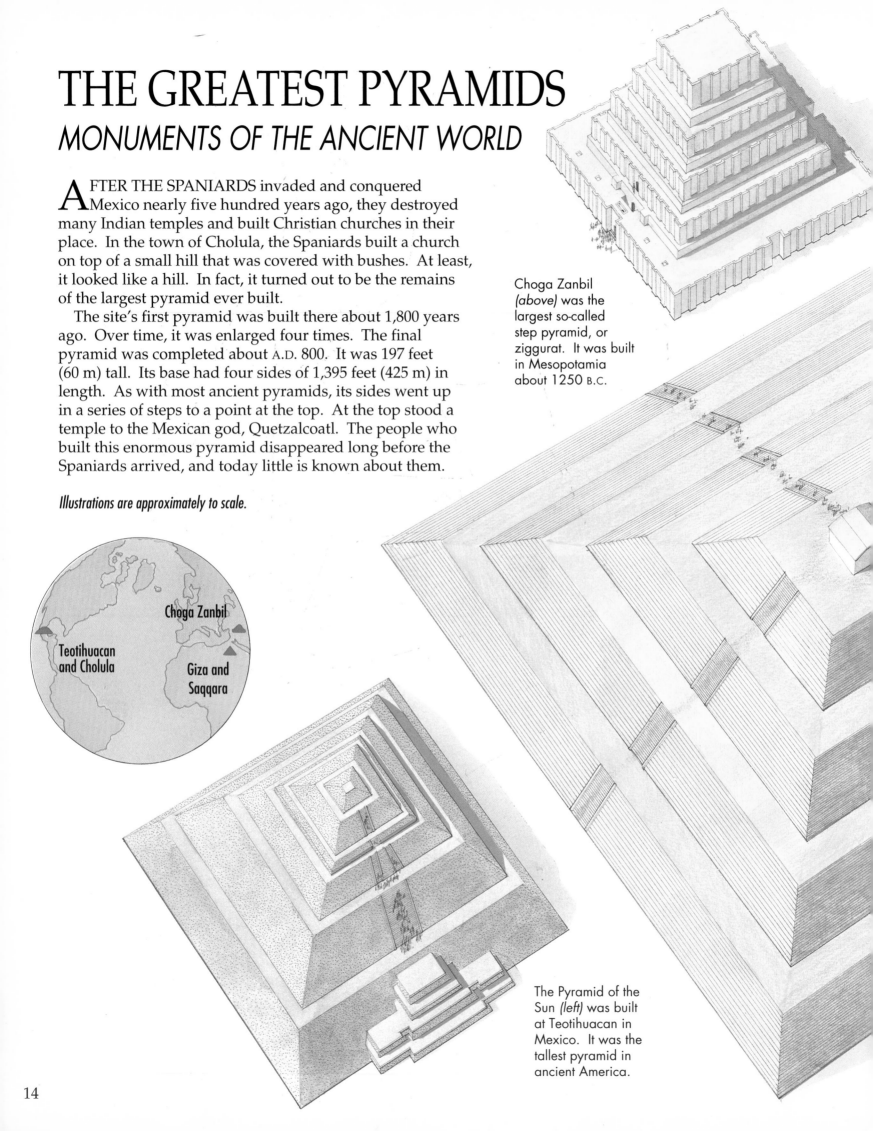

AFTER THE SPANIARDS invaded and conquered Mexico nearly five hundred years ago, they destroyed many Indian temples and built Christian churches in their place. In the town of Cholula, the Spaniards built a church on top of a small hill that was covered with bushes. At least, it looked like a hill. In fact, it turned out to be the remains of the largest pyramid ever built.

The site's first pyramid was built there about 1,800 years ago. Over time, it was enlarged four times. The final pyramid was completed about A.D. 800. It was 197 feet (60 m) tall. Its base had four sides of 1,395 feet (425 m) in length. As with most ancient pyramids, its sides went up in a series of steps to a point at the top. At the top stood a temple to the Mexican god, Quetzalcoatl. The people who built this enormous pyramid disappeared long before the Spaniards arrived, and today little is known about them.

Illustrations are approximately to scale.

Choga Zanbil *(above)* was the largest so-called step pyramid, or ziggurat. It was built in Mesopotamia about 1250 B.C.

Choga Zanbil

Teotihuacan and Cholula

Giza and Saqqara

The Pyramid of the Sun *(left)* was built at Teotihuacan in Mexico. It was the tallest pyramid in ancient America.

14

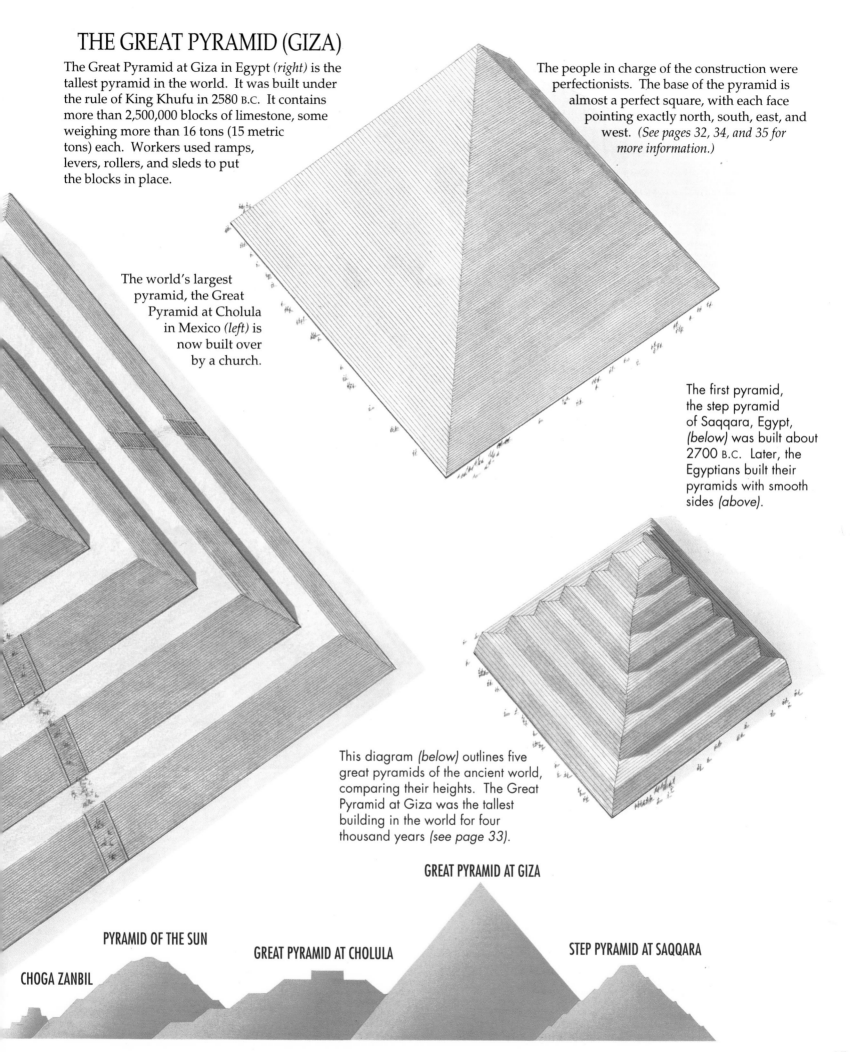

THE GREAT PYRAMID (GIZA)

The Great Pyramid at Giza in Egypt *(right)* is the tallest pyramid in the world. It was built under the rule of King Khufu in 2580 B.C. It contains more than 2,500,000 blocks of limestone, some weighing more than 16 tons (15 metric tons) each. Workers used ramps, levers, rollers, and sleds to put the blocks in place.

The world's largest pyramid, the Great Pyramid at Cholula in Mexico *(left)* is now built over by a church.

The people in charge of the construction were perfectionists. The base of the pyramid is almost a perfect square, with each face pointing exactly north, south, east, and west. *(See pages 32, 34, and 35 for more information.)*

The first pyramid, the step pyramid of Saqqara, Egypt, *(below)* was built about 2700 B.C. Later, the Egyptians built their pyramids with smooth sides *(above)*.

This diagram *(below)* outlines five great pyramids of the ancient world, comparing their heights. The Great Pyramid at Giza was the tallest building in the world for four thousand years *(see page 33)*.

GREAT PYRAMID AT GIZA

PYRAMID OF THE SUN

GREAT PYRAMID AT CHOLULA

STEP PYRAMID AT SAQQARA

CHOGA ZANBIL

THE GREATEST TEMPLES
THE WORLD'S LARGEST RELIGIOUS BUILDINGS

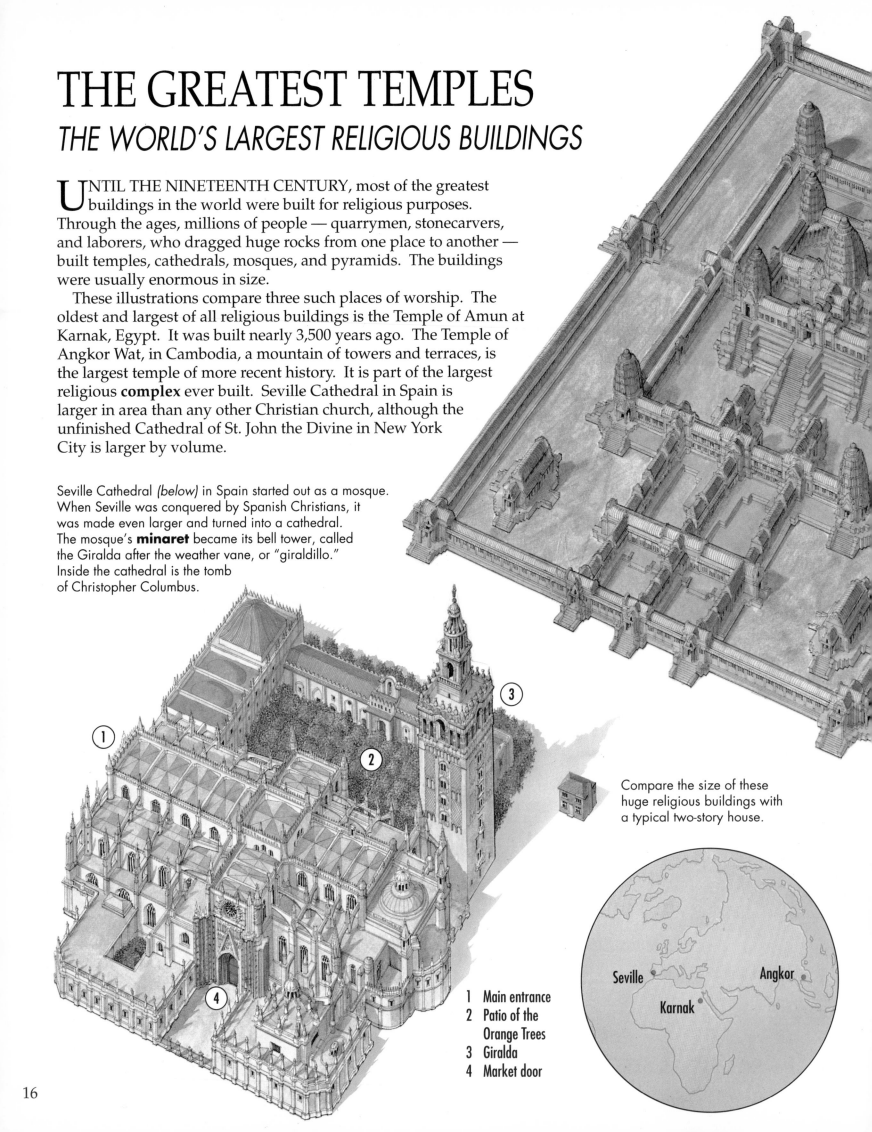

UNTIL THE NINETEENTH CENTURY, most of the greatest buildings in the world were built for religious purposes. Through the ages, millions of people — quarrymen, stonecarvers, and laborers, who dragged huge rocks from one place to another — built temples, cathedrals, mosques, and pyramids. The buildings were usually enormous in size.

These illustrations compare three such places of worship. The oldest and largest of all religious buildings is the Temple of Amun at Karnak, Egypt. It was built nearly 3,500 years ago. The Temple of Angkor Wat, in Cambodia, a mountain of towers and terraces, is the largest temple of more recent history. It is part of the largest religious **complex** ever built. Seville Cathedral in Spain is larger in area than any other Christian church, although the unfinished Cathedral of St. John the Divine in New York City is larger by volume.

Seville Cathedral *(below)* in Spain started out as a mosque. When Seville was conquered by Spanish Christians, it was made even larger and turned into a cathedral. The mosque's **minaret** became its bell tower, called the Giralda after the weather vane, or "giraldillo." Inside the cathedral is the tomb of Christopher Columbus.

Compare the size of these huge religious buildings with a typical two-story house.

1 Main entrance
2 Patio of the Orange Trees
3 Giralda
4 Market door

Seville   Angkor
Karnak

16

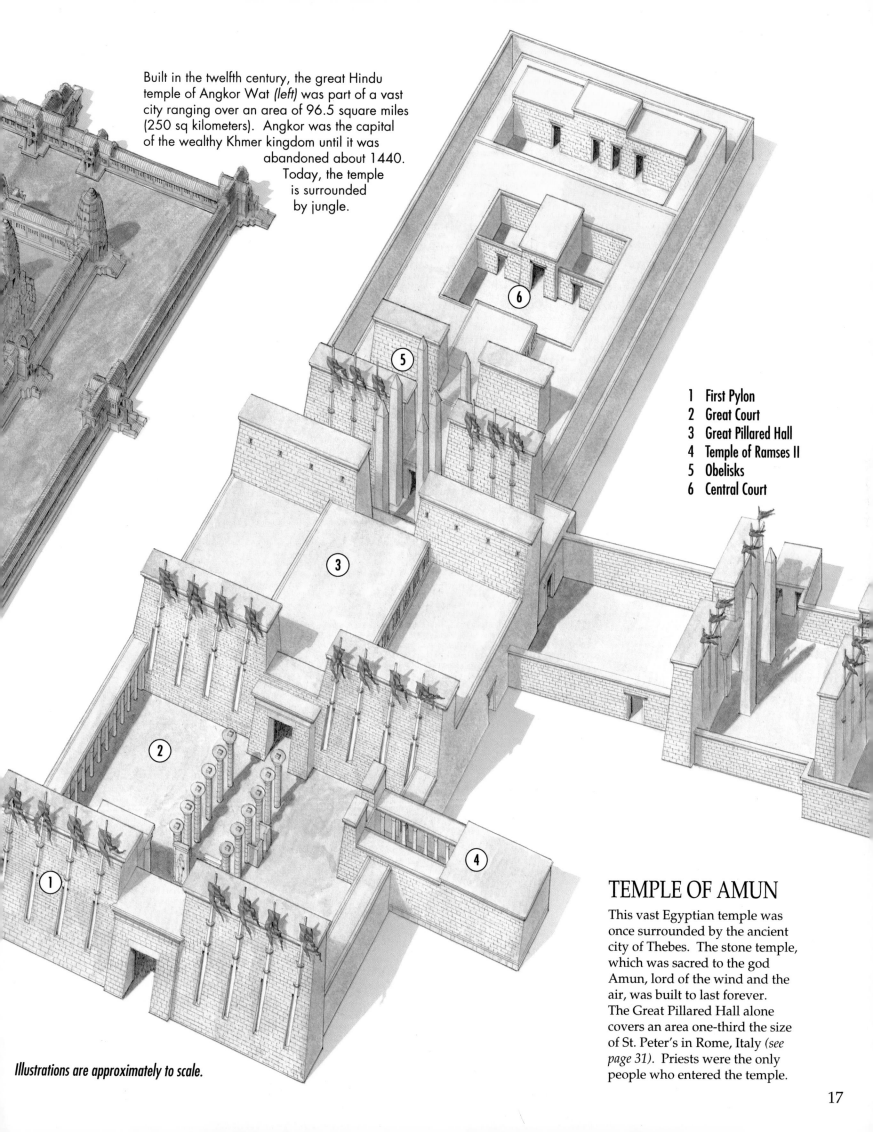

Built in the twelfth century, the great Hindu temple of Angkor Wat *(left)* was part of a vast city ranging over an area of 96.5 square miles (250 sq kilometers). Angkor was the capital of the wealthy Khmer kingdom until it was abandoned about 1440. Today, the temple is surrounded by jungle.

1 First Pylon
2 Great Court
3 Great Pillared Hall
4 Temple of Ramses II
5 Obelisks
6 Central Court

Illustrations are approximately to scale.

TEMPLE OF AMUN

This vast Egyptian temple was once surrounded by the ancient city of Thebes. The stone temple, which was sacred to the god Amun, lord of the wind and the air, was built to last forever. The Great Pillared Hall alone covers an area one-third the size of St. Peter's in Rome, Italy *(see page 31)*. Priests were the only people who entered the temple.

THE EARLIEST SPORTS
MARTIAL ARTS IN ANCIENT EGYPT

OUR EARLIEST ANCESTORS were hunters, but they hunted for food, not for sport. True sports did not begin until civilization was established, when kings and noblemen hunted wild animals with spears. They hunted because they enjoyed it, not because they needed the animals for food.

Many of the earliest sports, called the **martial arts**, were based on fighting. These sports included wrestling, archery, and fencing. Most of these sports originated when young men were trained for battle by practicing combat with their hands or with weapons.

Egypt was one of the first civilizations. A great deal is known about ancient Egypt because the early Egyptians left records of nearly everything they did, in both words and pictures. Paintings from the time depict young men wrestling or fencing. Writings describe swimming contests and rowing matches held on the Nile River.

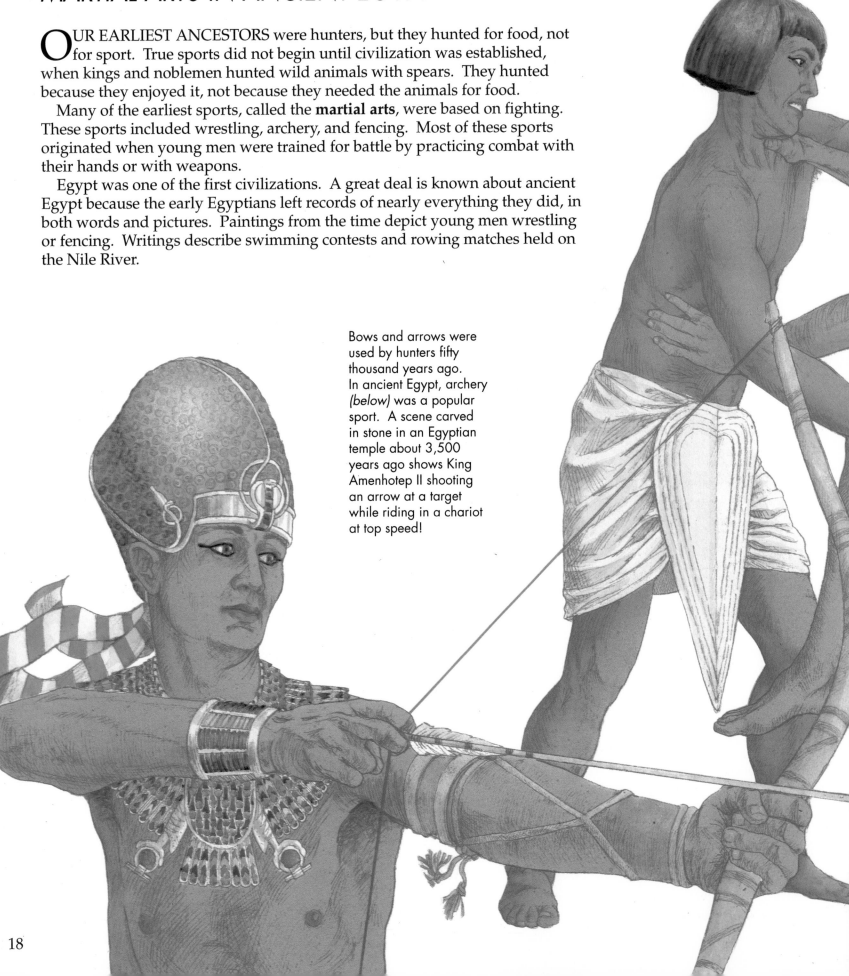

Bows and arrows were used by hunters fifty thousand years ago. In ancient Egypt, archery *(below)* was a popular sport. A scene carved in stone in an Egyptian temple about 3,500 years ago shows King Amenhotep II shooting an arrow at a target while riding in a chariot at top speed!

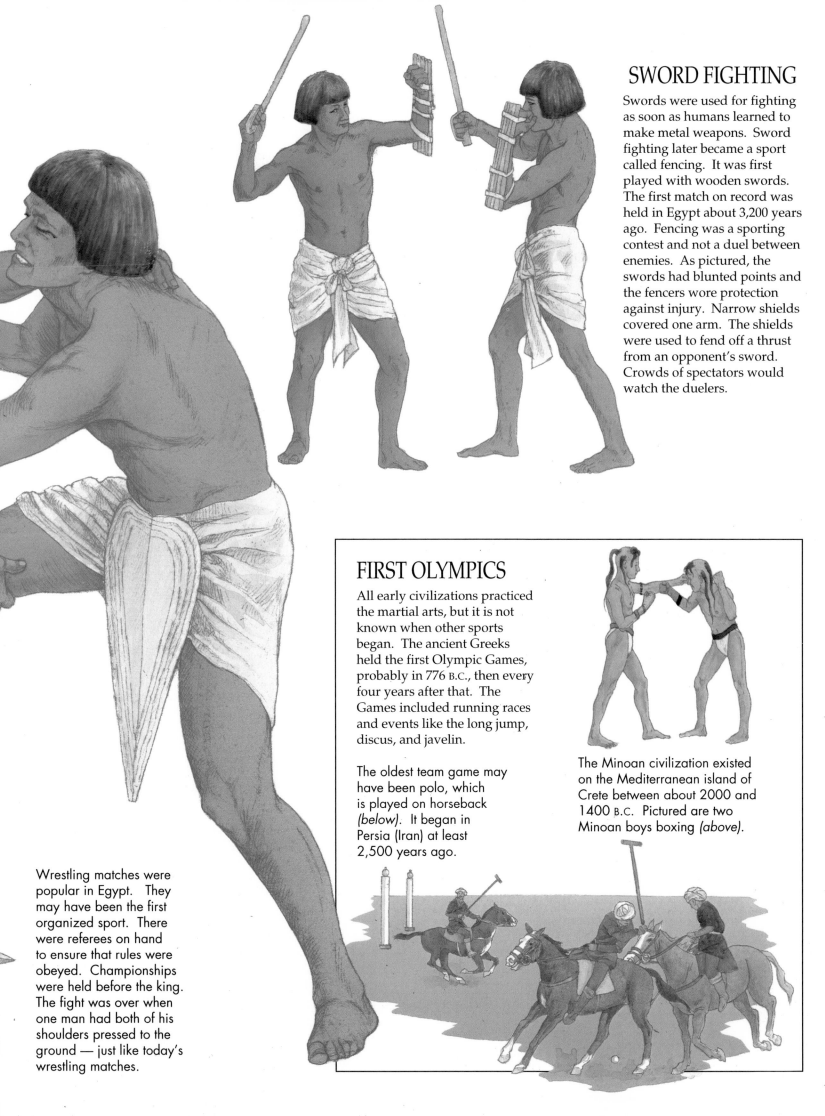

SWORD FIGHTING

Swords were used for fighting as soon as humans learned to make metal weapons. Sword fighting later became a sport called fencing. It was first played with wooden swords. The first match on record was held in Egypt about 3,200 years ago. Fencing was a sporting contest and not a duel between enemies. As pictured, the swords had blunted points and the fencers wore protection against injury. Narrow shields covered one arm. The shields were used to fend off a thrust from an opponent's sword. Crowds of spectators would watch the duelers.

FIRST OLYMPICS

All early civilizations practiced the martial arts, but it is not known when other sports began. The ancient Greeks held the first Olympic Games, probably in 776 B.C., then every four years after that. The Games included running races and events like the long jump, discus, and javelin.

The oldest team game may have been polo, which is played on horseback *(below)*. It began in Persia (Iran) at least 2,500 years ago.

The Minoan civilization existed on the Mediterranean island of Crete between about 2000 and 1400 B.C. Pictured are two Minoan boys boxing *(above)*.

Wrestling matches were popular in Egypt. They may have been the first organized sport. There were referees on hand to ensure that rules were obeyed. Championships were held before the king. The fight was over when one man had both of his shoulders pressed to the ground — just like today's wrestling matches.

THE LARGEST PALACE
INSIDE THE FORBIDDEN CITY

IMAGINE A BOX. Open it, and inside is another smaller box, inside that another, and so on. Beijing, the capital of China, is similar to this. It has an Inner City, the oldest part, and an Outer City in the form of a huge square. Inside the Inner City was the Imperial City, also in the shape of a square. Inside the Imperial City was yet another square, containing the Forbidden City. Within its walls were the palace buildings where the emperors lived until 1912. The last emperor, Puyi, a boy of six, **abdicated** but lived in the palace until 1924. The Forbidden City was named as such because the public was not allowed inside. If people disobeyed this rule, they were executed. Today, this largest palace in the world (within the Forbidden City) is open to the public.

Beijing

CHINA

Forbidden City marked in red

1 Meridian Gate
2 Gate of Supreme Harmony
3 Dragon Pavement
4 Hall of Supreme Harmony
5 Hall of Protecting Harmony
6 Palace of Heavenly Purity

Construction of the palace of the Forbidden City began under the Ming Emperor Yong Le *(left)* in 1404.

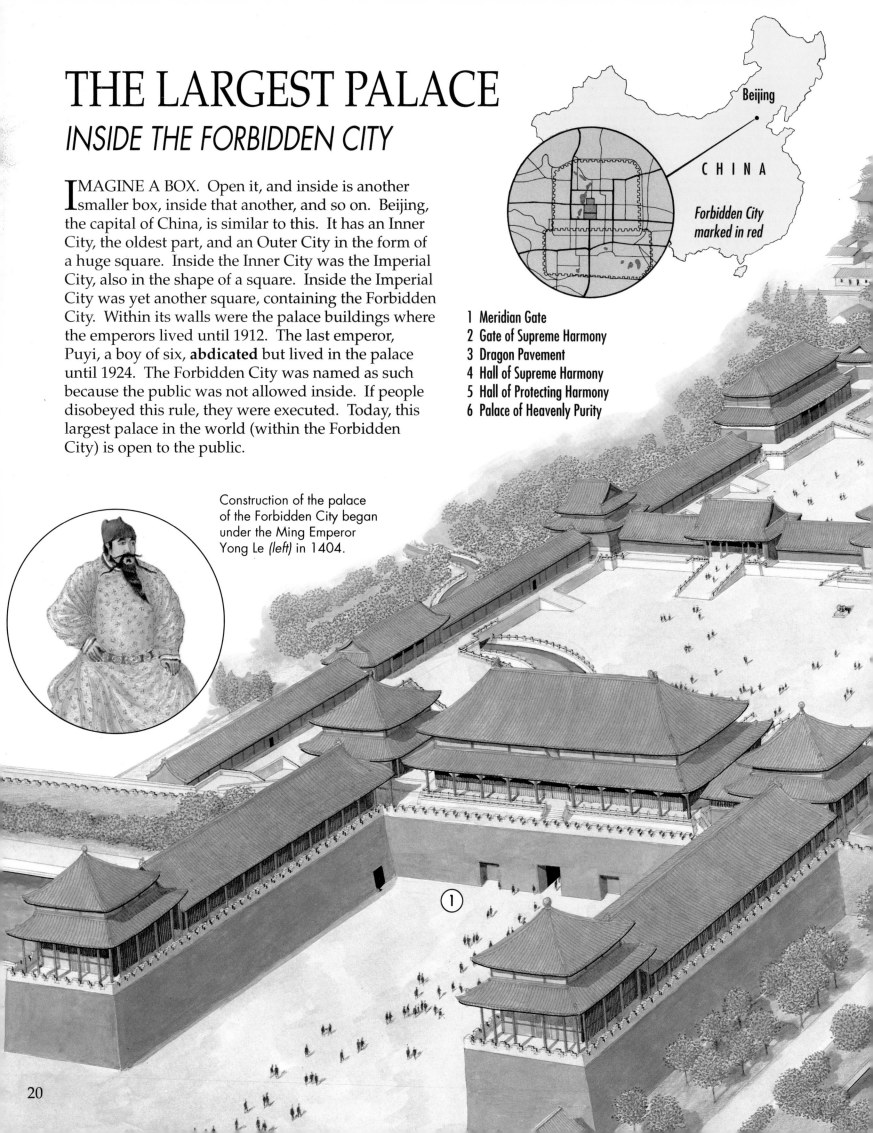

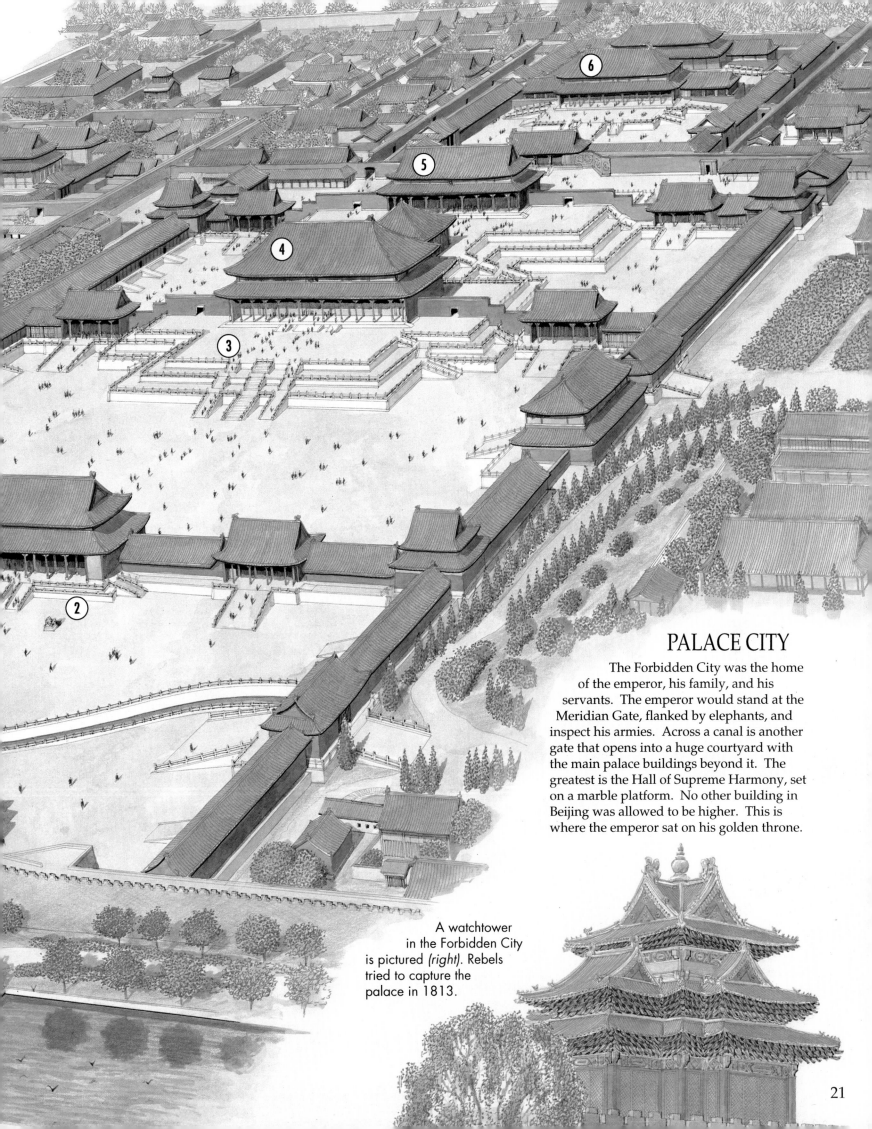

PALACE CITY

The Forbidden City was the home of the emperor, his family, and his servants. The emperor would stand at the Meridian Gate, flanked by elephants, and inspect his armies. Across a canal is another gate that opens into a huge courtyard with the main palace buildings beyond it. The greatest is the Hall of Supreme Harmony, set on a marble platform. No other building in Beijing was allowed to be higher. This is where the emperor sat on his golden throne.

A watchtower in the Forbidden City is pictured *(right)*. Rebels tried to capture the palace in 1813.

THE LONGEST WALL
THE GREAT WALL OF CHINA

The Chinese thought of the Great Wall as a dragon *(right)* that defended their country against the warlike tribes that lived to the north.

DEFENDING THE WALL

The soldiers who guarded the wall lived in the towers. When an attack came, they lit a fire as a signal to other soldiers. Then soldiers from other parts of the wall rushed to help. They fired arrows down on the enemy warriors trying to climb the wall. They also launched stones from giant catapults. In peaceful times, the soldiers repaired the wall or worked the fields in the area.

Great Wall

CHINA

THE FIRST GREAT WALL

TEN THOUSAND YEARS AGO, nearly all humans were nomads. They moved from place to place with their herds, living off the land. In a few places, people learned to grow crops. They were able to settle down in villages. They built permanent houses, learned new crafts (such as metalwork), and traded with other villages. What is known as civilization then began. To some of the people who remained nomads, the villages were tempting targets. The nomads raided the villages for food. They killed the people and burned the houses. To keep the raiders out, villagers built walls around their settlements. One of the earliest centers of civilization was northern China. By 200 B.C., a large region was ruled by the emperors of the Qin dynasty. It was often raided by the Huns, a fierce race of nomads. The Qin emperors decided to build a long wall to keep them out. This was the first Great Wall of China. It ran from the Yellow Sea to the deserts of Central Asia.

The Great Wall snakes across China's mountains and valleys. In some places, such as the gate at Xifengkou Pass near the eastern end, the wall is three walls deep. Extra fortification was built at certain points such as this.

BUILDING THE WALL

The Great Wall is the largest construction project ever undertaken. The construction lasted for centuries. Most of the present wall was built in the 14th-16th centuries. Millions of men worked on it, carrying the stone in baskets *(right)*. The final length was over 3,700 miles (6,000 km) (more than two-thirds the distance across the United States). The wall is almost 33 feet (10 m) high, with towers every 656 feet (200 m). It is wide enough for ten people to walk on, side-by-side.

THE OLDEST MONARCHY
JAPAN'S EMPERORS

THE PEOPLE OF ANCIENT JAPAN believed the islands of their country were created by the goddess of the Sun. They believed a man named Jimmu was a child of the Sun goddess. He united Japan under his rule and became the first emperor.

The **legends** say Jimmu's rule began in 660 B.C. Modern historians are not so sure. They think Jimmu may have lived hundreds of years later, from about 40 B.C. to 10 B.C. In any event, the same imperial family has ruled Japan to the present day. No other **monarchy** in the world has lasted as long.

Japan has always had an emperor, or sometimes an empress, who was looked upon as a god as well as a monarch. But the god-emperor was not always a powerful ruler. For hundreds of years, other great families, stronger than the royal family, fought for control. Japan was torn by civil wars.

Japan became a settled, peaceful country in the sixteenth century. The people who brought peace were the **shoguns**, or governors, of the Tokugawa family. Though loyal to the emperor, they held all the power. For two hundred years, they closed the country. Few foreigners were allowed in, and no Japanese were allowed out. There was peace. Warlike nobles were kept in their castles. The emperors lived quietly in their palace in Kyoto.

Emperor Jimmu *(right)* and his descendants united the Japanese islands over two thousand years ago. His life and deeds are part of legend.

Prince Shotoku built the first Buddhist monasteries. The one called Horyuji at Nara *(right)* is the oldest surviving wooden building in the world.

The Japanese religion of Shinto was founded by the Emperor Suinin about 1,500 years ago. Pictured *(left)* is the first Shinto shrine, or temple, at Ise. Emperor Suinin built the shrine for the Sun goddess. Inside the building, he placed her sacred mirror that is still there today.

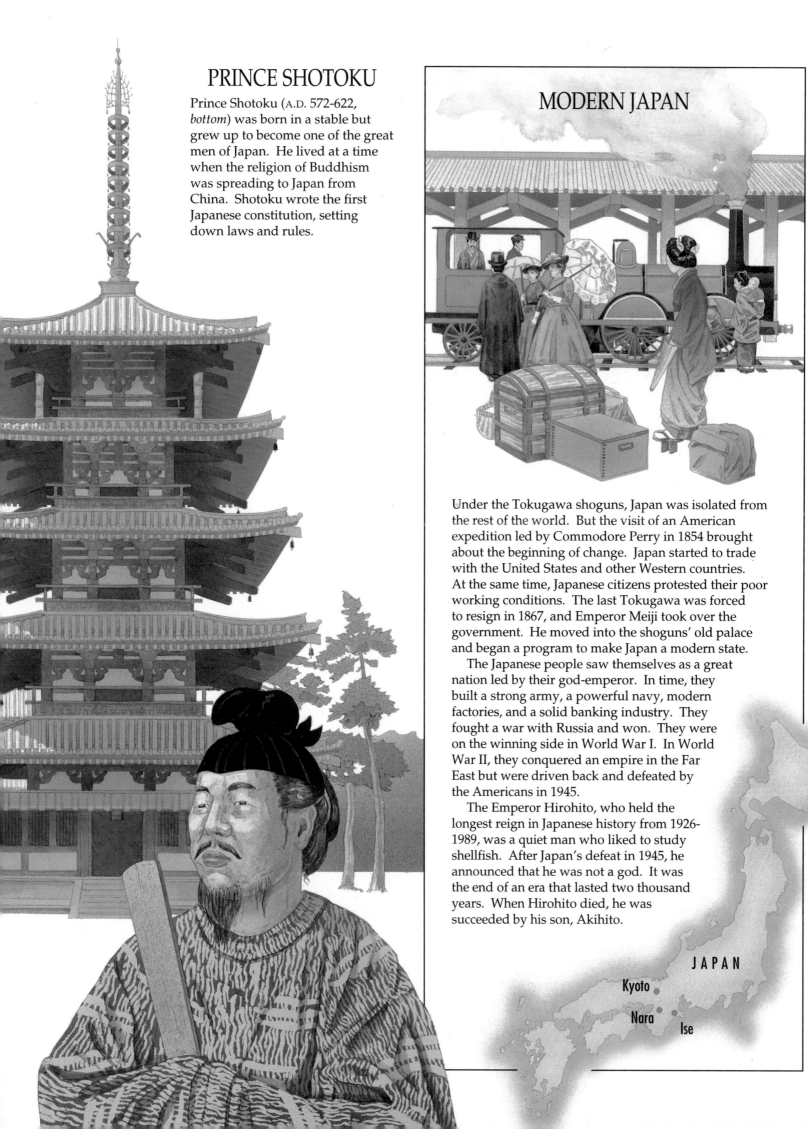

PRINCE SHOTOKU

Prince Shotoku (A.D. 572-622, *bottom*) was born in a stable but grew up to become one of the great men of Japan. He lived at a time when the religion of Buddhism was spreading to Japan from China. Shotoku wrote the first Japanese constitution, setting down laws and rules.

MODERN JAPAN

Under the Tokugawa shoguns, Japan was isolated from the rest of the world. But the visit of an American expedition led by Commodore Perry in 1854 brought about the beginning of change. Japan started to trade with the United States and other Western countries. At the same time, Japanese citizens protested their poor working conditions. The last Tokugawa was forced to resign in 1867, and Emperor Meiji took over the government. He moved into the shoguns' old palace and began a program to make Japan a modern state.

The Japanese people saw themselves as a great nation led by their god-emperor. In time, they built a strong army, a powerful navy, modern factories, and a solid banking industry. They fought a war with Russia and won. They were on the winning side in World War I. In World War II, they conquered an empire in the Far East but were driven back and defeated by the Americans in 1945.

The Emperor Hirohito, who held the longest reign in Japanese history from 1926-1989, was a quiet man who liked to study shellfish. After Japan's defeat in 1945, he announced that he was not a god. It was the end of an era that lasted two thousand years. When Hirohito died, he was succeeded by his son, Akihito.

JAPAN

Kyoto

Nara

Ise

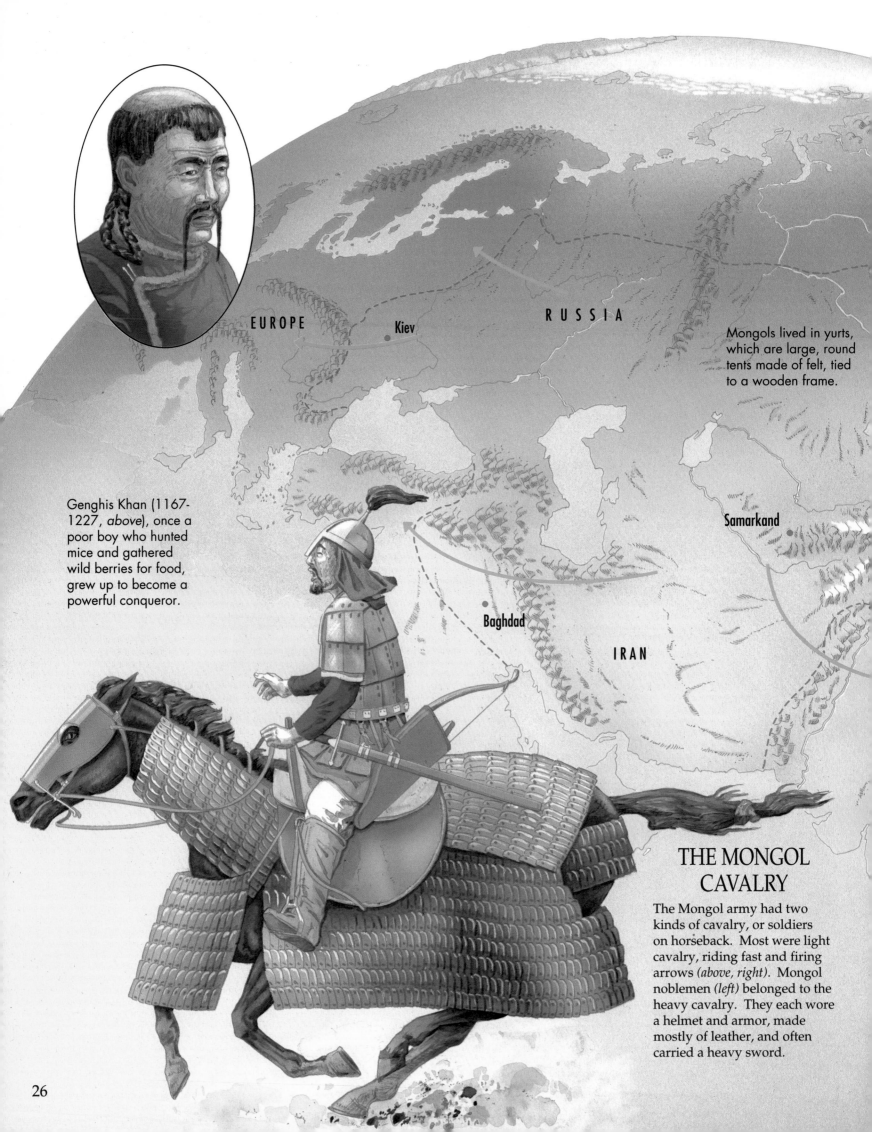

EUROPE

RUSSIA

Kiev

Mongols lived in yurts, which are large, round tents made of felt, tied to a wooden frame.

Genghis Khan (1167-1227, *above*), once a poor boy who hunted mice and gathered wild berries for food, grew up to become a powerful conqueror.

Samarkand

Baghdad

IRAN

THE MONGOL CAVALRY

The Mongol army had two kinds of cavalry, or soldiers on horseback. Most were light cavalry, riding fast and firing arrows (*above, right*). Mongol noblemen (*left*) belonged to the heavy cavalry. They each wore a helmet and armor, made mostly of leather, and often carried a heavy sword.

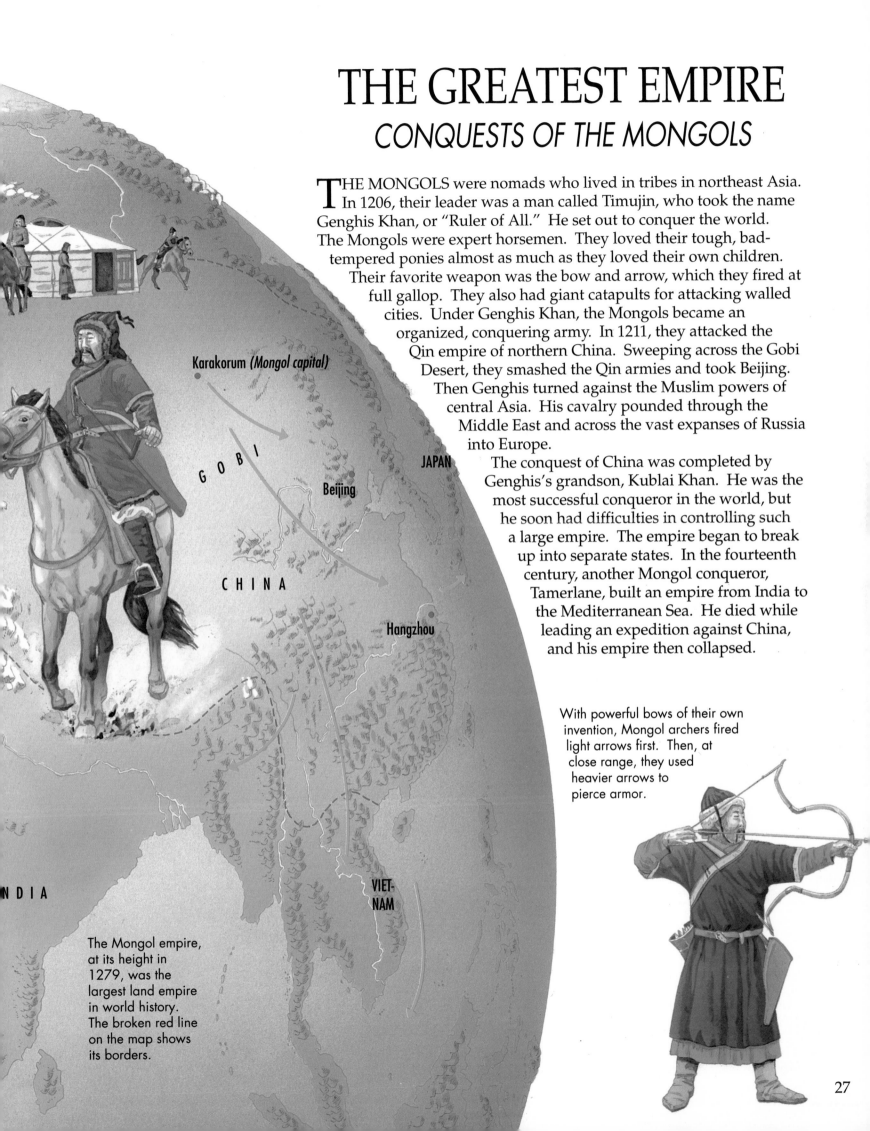

THE GREATEST EMPIRE
CONQUESTS OF THE MONGOLS

THE MONGOLS were nomads who lived in tribes in northeast Asia. In 1206, their leader was a man called Timujin, who took the name Genghis Khan, or "Ruler of All." He set out to conquer the world. The Mongols were expert horsemen. They loved their tough, bad-tempered ponies almost as much as they loved their own children. Their favorite weapon was the bow and arrow, which they fired at full gallop. They also had giant catapults for attacking walled cities. Under Genghis Khan, the Mongols became an organized, conquering army. In 1211, they attacked the Qin empire of northern China. Sweeping across the Gobi Desert, they smashed the Qin armies and took Beijing. Then Genghis turned against the Muslim powers of central Asia. His cavalry pounded through the Middle East and across the vast expanses of Russia into Europe.

The conquest of China was completed by Genghis's grandson, Kublai Khan. He was the most successful conqueror in the world, but he soon had difficulties in controlling such a large empire. The empire began to break up into separate states. In the fourteenth century, another Mongol conqueror, Tamerlane, built an empire from India to the Mediterranean Sea. He died while leading an expedition against China, and his empire then collapsed.

Karakorum *(Mongol capital)*

GOBI

CHINA

JAPAN

Beijing

Hangzhou

VIET-NAM

INDIA

The Mongol empire, at its height in 1279, was the largest land empire in world history. The broken red line on the map shows its borders.

With powerful bows of their own invention, Mongol archers fired light arrows first. Then, at close range, they used heavier arrows to pierce armor.

27

THE LARGEST CASTLE
PRAGUE CASTLE, HEART OF THE CZECH LANDS

PRAGUE CASTLE is the Czechs's greatest national monument. It is also the largest ancient castle in the world. Known to the Czechs as Hradcany, it was built by a prince in the ninth century. It has been rebuilt and enlarged many times since then. Today, it has an area of 66 acres (26.7 hectares). The castle is like a town inside a town. There is a group of buildings — palaces, churches, houses, and towers — all built in different centuries. Saint Vaclav, patron saint of the Czechs, also known as Good King Wenceslas, is buried there.

Prague Castle stands on a hill above the Vltava River, overlooking the city of Prague. Originally a wooden fortress, the castle contains buildings that date from the Middle Ages. Work on St. Vitus's Cathedral (center area) began a thousand years ago but was not finished until the twentieth century.

1 First Castle Courtyard
2 Second Castle Courtyard
3 St. Vitus's Cathedral
4 The Old Royal Palace
5 St. George's Basilica
6 Golden Lane
7 Daliborka Tower
8 The Black Tower

Windsor

Prague

WINDSOR CASTLE

Windsor Castle, near London in England, is the largest and oldest castle still used as a home. It is home to the Queen of England. It was first built by William the Conqueror to defend London in case of enemy attack along the valley of the Thames River. Inside the castle is a doll's house given to Queen Mary in 1924. It has tiny light bulbs the size of dewdrops and tiny cars that run 93,210 miles (150,000 km) on one gallon of gas!

THE SMALLEST COUNTRY
VATICAN CITY STATE

THE VATICAN CITY STATE is all that remains of lands belonging to the pope that, until 1870, included most of central Italy. Under an agreement made with the Italian government in 1929, the Vatican became a fully independent state with its own government. With an area of 109 acres (44 ha), it is the smallest independent country in the world.

The Vatican is the center of the Roman Catholic church, which numbers nearly 900 million followers. It is home to the pope, who is head of the Roman Catholic church, and 800 other people — the lowest population of any nation.

This tiny country is dominated by the magnificent St. Peter's Basilica (not a cathedral, but an important Roman Catholic church) and its square. The Vatican houses palaces, museums, colleges, two churches besides St. Peter's, and a railroad station. It runs its own bank, post office, and newspaper, and issues its own stamps and coins.

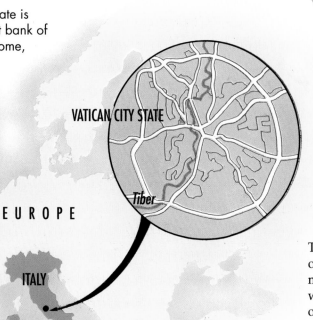

The Vatican City State is located on the west bank of the Tiber River in Rome, capital city of Italy.

VATICAN CITY STATE

Tiber

EUROPE

ITALY

Rome

THE OLDEST ARMY

The Swiss Guard, the official guard unit of the Vatican, was founded in 1506, making it the oldest existing army in the world. It is also the smallest, numbering one hundred. Members are Swiss and trained by the Swiss army. Only once did the Guard go to battle. In 1527, it fought the forces of Emperor Charles V.

THE LARGEST CHURCH

Where St. Peter's Basilica stands today was once called the Gardens of Nero. Many Christians were put to death there. They included St. Peter, one of Jesus's apostles, who died about A.D. 67. A church was later built over St. Peter's tomb. It stood for a thousand years before the popes decided they needed a new church to replace the crumbling old one. The greatest architects of the time, including Michelangelo, were hired to design and build the new St. Peter's. Begun in 1507, it took more than 150 years to complete. A church called the Basilica of Our Lady of Peace, built in Ivory Coast, Africa, in 1989, is taller but not as large as St. Peter's. Today, crowds gather in St. Peter's Square every week to receive the pope's blessing, which he delivers from a balcony overlooking the square.

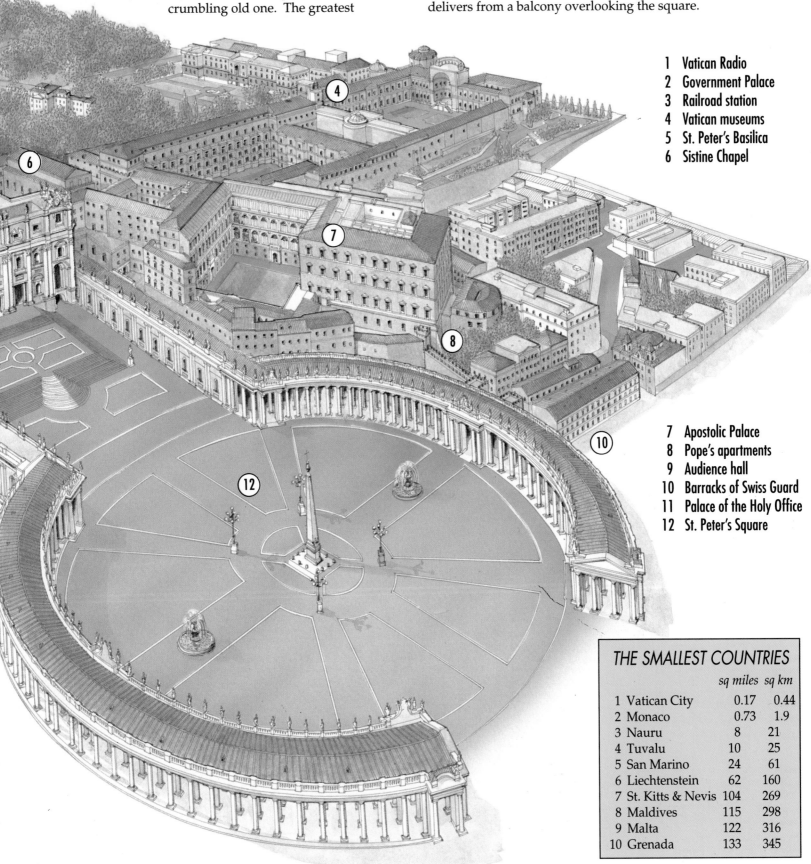

1 Vatican Radio
2 Government Palace
3 Railroad station
4 Vatican museums
5 St. Peter's Basilica
6 Sistine Chapel

7 Apostolic Palace
8 Pope's apartments
9 Audience hall
10 Barracks of Swiss Guard
11 Palace of the Holy Office
12 St. Peter's Square

THE SMALLEST COUNTRIES

		sq miles	sq km
1	Vatican City	0.17	0.44
2	Monaco	0.73	1.9
3	Nauru	8	21
4	Tuvalu	10	25
5	San Marino	24	61
6	Liechtenstein	62	160
7	St. Kitts & Nevis	104	269
8	Maldives	115	298
9	Malta	122	316
10	Grenada	133	345

REACHING FOR THE SKIES
THE WORLD'S TALLEST BUILDINGS

FOR NEARLY FOUR THOUSAND YEARS, the Great Pyramid of Giza stood taller than all the other great pyramids of ancient Egypt — and every other building in the world. It is the only one of the so-called Seven Wonders of the World to survive mostly intact. It lost 33 feet (10 m) off its height when the topmost stones fell away (see page 15).

When the great cathedrals of medieval Europe were built, the Great Pyramid was no longer the tallest structure. In 1311, the central tower of Lincoln Cathedral in England, topped by a lead-covered wooden spire, finally outreached the Great Pyramid. Although the spire blew down in a storm in 1549, no higher building was erected until the Washington Monument in 1884. It honored the first president of the United States, George Washington.

Just five years later, the record returned to Europe. Gustav Eiffel's iron tower, the marvel of the 1889 Paris International Exhibition in France, astonished the world. It took 230 men just over two years to build the Eiffel Tower, hammering together 18,000 pieces of iron using 2,500,000 rivets. Extended in 1959 by a 66-foot (20-m) television antenna, the Eiffel Tower sways up to 5 inches (13 cm) in high winds. In hot weather, the metal expands and the tower grows another 7 inches (18 cm) taller.

The **skyscraper** was made possible by the use of steel building frames and the invention of hydraulic lifts. In 1930, the Chrysler Building in New York City became the world's tallest building. It was overtaken by another New York skyscraper, the Empire State Building, a few months later. The Empire State's spire, extended by a television mast twenty years later, was originally intended to be a mooring post for airships. It remained the world's tallest building until 1973, when the twin towers of the World Trade Center, also in New York City, were built.

The record quickly changed hands. Chicago took the record later in 1973 with its Sears Tower. In 1976, the CN Tower in Toronto became the world's tallest self-supporting structure. The 96-story Petronas Twin Towers (not pictured) in Kuala Lumpur, Malaysia, became the world's tallest buildings in 1997.

Illustrations are approximately to scale.

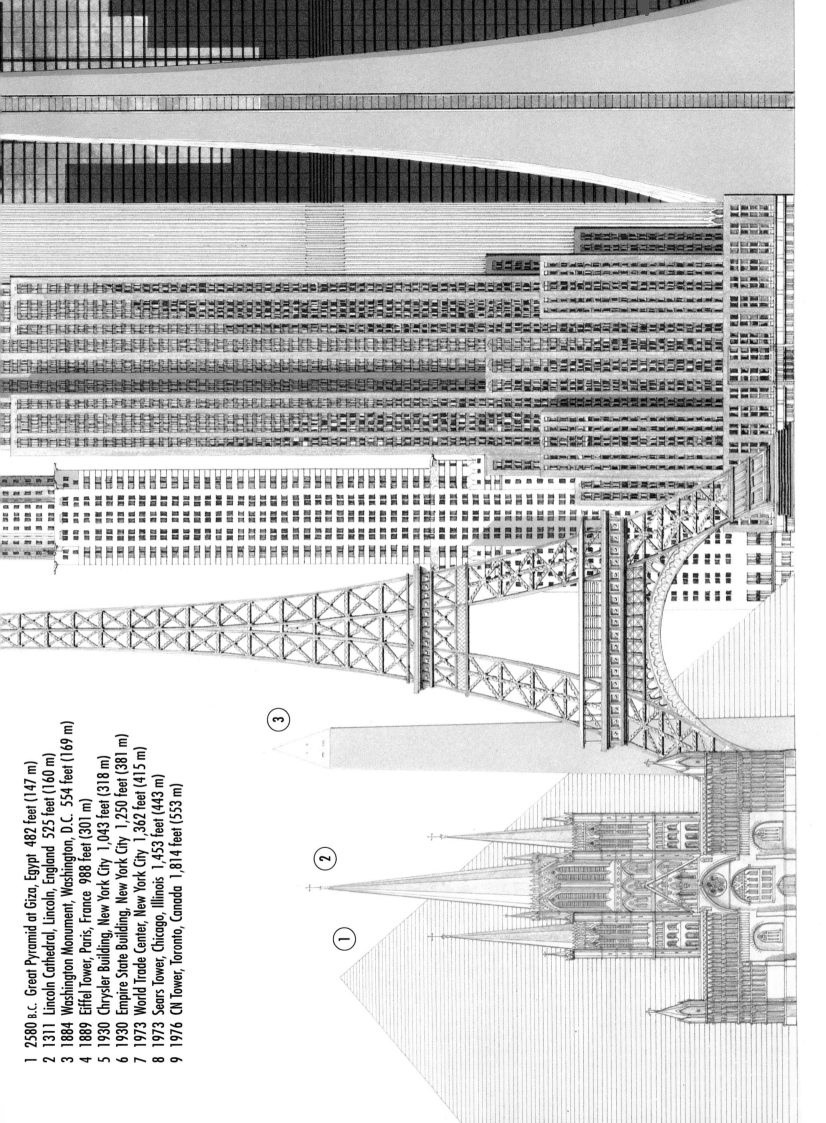

1 2580 B.C. Great Pyramid at Giza, Egypt 482 feet (147 m)
2 1311 Lincoln Cathedral, Lincoln, England 525 feet (160 m)
3 1884 Washington Monument, Washington, D.C. 554 feet (169 m)
4 1889 Eiffel Tower, Paris, France 988 feet (301 m)
5 1930 Chrysler Building, New York City 1,043 feet (318 m)
6 1930 Empire State Building, New York City 1,250 feet (381 m)
7 1973 World Trade Center, New York City 1,362 feet (415 m)
8 1973 Sears Tower, Chicago, Illinois 1,453 feet (443 m)
9 1976 CN Tower, Toronto, Canada 1,814 feet (553 m)

THE TALLEST MONUMENTS
AND THE TALLEST STEEPLE

GATEWAY ARCH, the tallest monument in the world, stands on the banks of the Mississippi River in the city of St. Louis, Missouri. Built in 1965, the 630-foot (192-m)- tall stainless steel arch was designed in the shape of a rainbow. The arch is hollow inside. Elevators go to the top where there are portholes to view the city.

The Gateway Arch marks St. Louis's historic role as "gateway to the West." In the mid-nineteenth century, farmers and others, their wagon trains laden with possessions and drawn by oxen, set out from St. Louis bound for Oregon and California. These adventurous people hoped for a better life in the American West.

THE LARGEST SCULPTURE

Mount Rushmore in the Black Hills of South Dakota is the largest completed sculpture in the world. Carved into a mountain are 66-foot (20-m)- tall stone heads of American presidents George Washington, Thomas Jefferson, Theodore Roosevelt, and Abraham Lincoln. The sculpture was carved by Gutzon Borglum and his assistants in 1927-1941.

The Mount Rushmore presidents will someday be dwarfed by a statue of the great American Indian chief, Crazy Horse. The statue, carved by Korczak Ziolkowski and his assistants, will be 564 feet (172 m) tall upon completion. Carving began in the Black Hills, lands sacred to the Sioux, not far from Mount Rushmore, in 1948. Crazy Horse was one of the greatest warriors and chiefs of the Oglala Sioux Indians. He led a resistance to the forced removal of his people from the Black Hills onto a reservation, defending his people and their way of life.

Illustrations are approximately to scale.

GATEWAY ARCH

ULM CATHEDRAL

The Cathedral, or Munster, at Ulm, Germany, has the tallest church steeple. From the laying of its foundations to the completion of its spire, the building took five hundred years to complete.

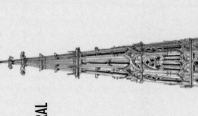

SAN JACINTO MONUMENT

The highest column in the world is at San Jacinto, Texas *(left)*. It is 571 feet (174 m) tall. The Texas star at the top weighs nearly 220 tons (200 metric tons). The column was built in 1936 to commemorate a battle fought one hundred years earlier. In an attack lasting only eighteen minutes, Texan soldiers defeated the Mexican army. For the next nine years, until 1845, Texas was an independent nation.

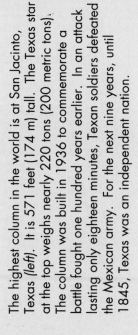

GREAT PYRAMID AT GIZA
482 feet (147 m)
Tallest pyramid

COAST REDWOOD
394 feet (120 m)
Tallest tree

The tallest statue in the world is the bronze Amida Buddha in Ushiku City, Japan.

AMIDA BUDDHA
394 feet (120 m)
Tallest statue

35

THE LONGEST BRIDGE

JAPAN'S HONSHU-SHIKOKU BRIDGE PROJECT

JAPAN IS A COUNTRY of islands. It has four large islands and hundreds of small ones. By the time the Honshu-Shikoku Bridge Project is complete, people will be able to drive or travel by train to all four main islands. The islands will be linked by bridges or tunnels.

The project consists of three crossings, each made up of a number of bridges linked together in a chain (*inset*). One crossing has already been built, and the others will be finished by the end of the twentieth century. One of the three will include the Akashi-Kaikyo Bridge. When completed, it will be the longest suspension bridge in the world, taking the record held by the Humber Bridge in England.

The stretch of water that the bridges cross is called the Seto Inland Sea. It has many small islands, some of which have been used as "stepping stones" for the bridge supports.

Because the seabed is hard granite, supports can also be built in the water. The bridges must be able to stand up against Japan's earthquakes and **typhoons**, as well as strong tidal currents in the Seto Inland Sea. The bridge engineers also had to keep in mind that this region is a national park, where rare and beautiful plants and animals live. They had to plan the bridges and roads in a way that would not harm the environment.

JAPAN

Area of inset (*below*)

Iwakurojima Bridge

Yoshima Bridge

Yoshima Viaduct

Minami Bisan-seto Bridge

Kita Bisan-seto Bridge

OSAKA

KOBE

Akashi-Kaikyo Bridge

SETO INLAND SEA

HONSHU

Onomichi-Imabari Bridge

Seto-Ohashi Bridge

SHIKOKU

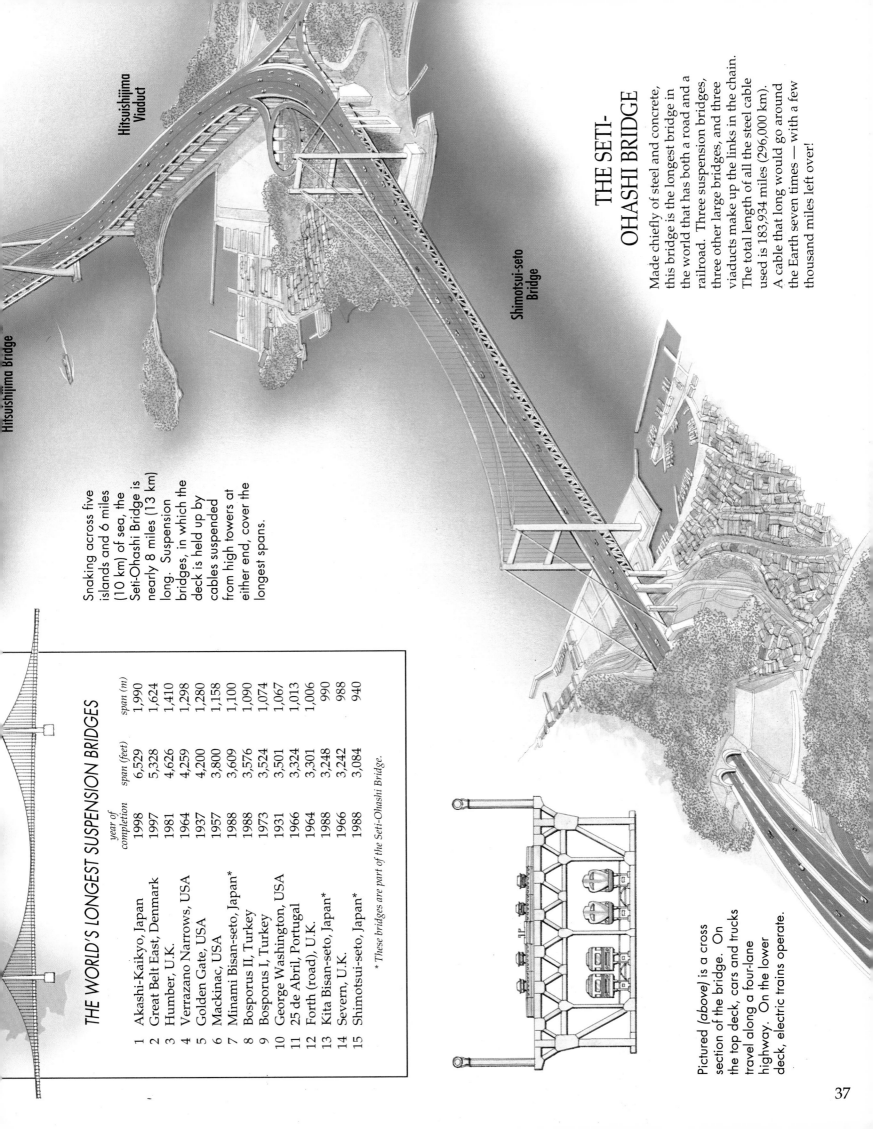

Hitsuishijima Viaduct

Hitsuishijima Bridge

Shimotsui-seto Bridge

THE SETI-OHASHI BRIDGE

Made chiefly of steel and concrete, this bridge is the longest bridge in the world that has both a road and a railroad. Three suspension bridges, three other large bridges, and three viaducts make up the links in the chain. The total length of all the steel cable used is 183,934 miles (296,000 km). A cable that long would go around the Earth seven times — with a few thousand miles left over!

Snaking across five islands and 6 miles (10 km) of sea, the Seti-Ohashi Bridge is nearly 8 miles (13 km) long. Suspension bridges, in which the deck is held up by cables suspended from high towers at either end, cover the longest spans.

THE WORLD'S LONGEST SUSPENSION BRIDGES

		year of completion	span (feet)	span (m)
1	Akashi-Kaikyo, Japan	1998	6,529	1,990
2	Great Belt East, Denmark	1997	5,328	1,624
3	Humber, U.K.	1981	4,626	1,410
4	Verrazano Narrows, USA	1964	4,259	1,298
5	Golden Gate, USA	1937	4,200	1,280
6	Mackinac, USA	1957	3,800	1,158
7	Minami Bisan-seto, Japan*	1988	3,609	1,100
8	Bosporus II, Turkey	1988	3,576	1,090
9	Bosporus I, Turkey	1973	3,524	1,074
10	George Washington, USA	1931	3,501	1,067
11	25 de Abril, Portugal	1966	3,324	1,013
12	Forth (road), U.K.	1964	3,301	1,006
13	Kita Bisan-seto, Japan*	1988	3,248	990
14	Severn, U.K.	1966	3,242	988
15	Shimotsui-seto, Japan*	1988	3,084	940

These bridges are part of the Seti-Ohashi Bridge.

Pictured (above) is a cross section of the bridge. On the top deck, cars and trucks travel along a four-lane highway. On the lower deck, electric trains operate.

37

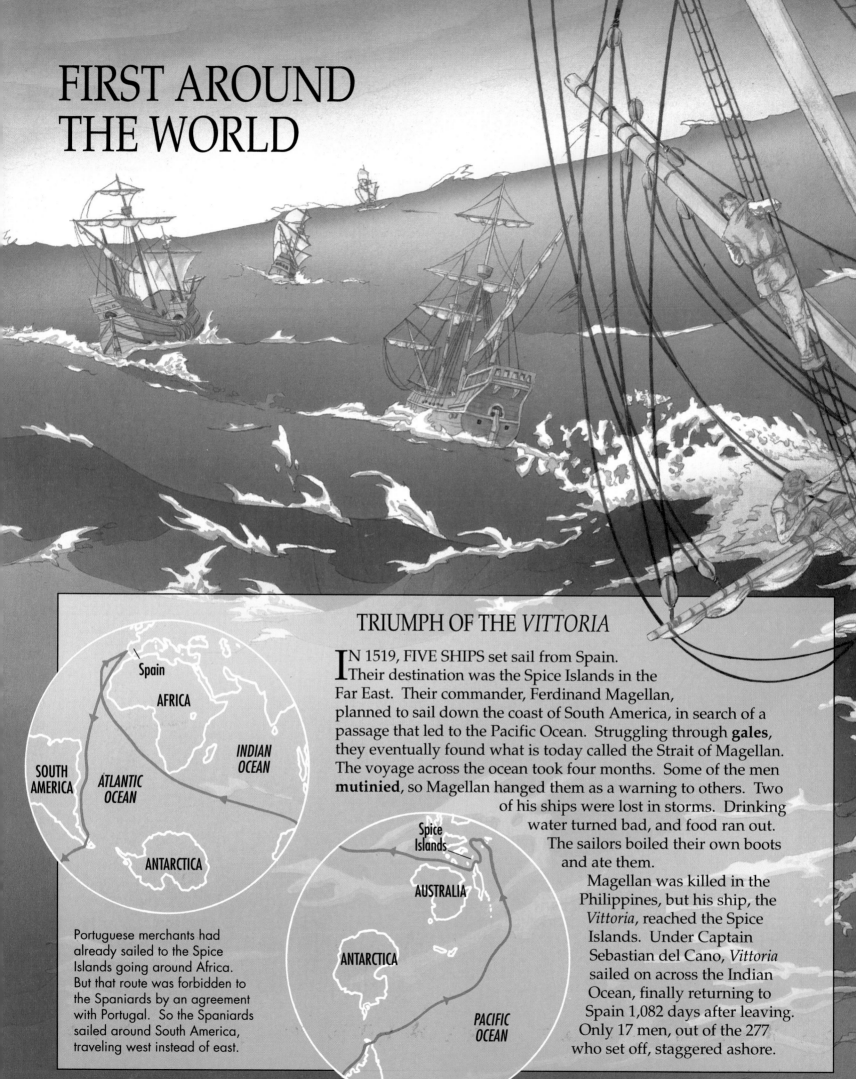

FIRST AROUND THE WORLD

TRIUMPH OF THE *VITTORIA*

IN 1519, FIVE SHIPS set sail from Spain. Their destination was the Spice Islands in the Far East. Their commander, Ferdinand Magellan, planned to sail down the coast of South America, in search of a passage that led to the Pacific Ocean. Struggling through **gales**, they eventually found what is today called the Strait of Magellan. The voyage across the ocean took four months. Some of the men **mutinied**, so Magellan hanged them as a warning to others. Two of his ships were lost in storms. Drinking water turned bad, and food ran out. The sailors boiled their own boots and ate them.

Magellan was killed in the Philippines, but his ship, the *Vittoria*, reached the Spice Islands. Under Captain Sebastian del Cano, *Vittoria* sailed on across the Indian Ocean, finally returning to Spain 1,082 days after leaving. Only 17 men, out of the 277 who set off, staggered ashore.

Portuguese merchants had already sailed to the Spice Islands going around Africa. But that route was forbidden to the Spaniards by an agreement with Portugal. So the Spaniards sailed around South America, traveling west instead of east.

Spain
AFRICA
INDIAN OCEAN
SOUTH AMERICA
ATLANTIC OCEAN
ANTARCTICA

Spice Islands
AUSTRALIA
ANTARCTICA
PACIFIC OCEAN

ARCTIC OCEAN

North Pole

GREENLAND

Peary's route 1908-1909

Robert E. Peary (1856-1920) helped build the Panama Canal before he became a polar explorer. He spent years with the Inuit people, learning how to live in the Arctic.

Robert Peary and some of his team are pictured near the place Peary claimed to be the North Pole. The American flag is planted in a mound of snow.

IN 1909, AMERICAN EXPLORER Robert Peary began his eighth Arctic expedition. He was determined to reach the North Pole.

From his base on Cape Columbia in the Canadian Arctic, Peary set out with nineteen dog sleds and a team of explorers that included African-American Matthew Henson and four Inuit. They traveled across the shifting, broken ice of the Arctic Ocean. Although often held up by stretches of open water, they advanced at a rate of 15 miles (24 km) a day. On April 6, they claimed to have reached the North Pole.

In the final dash, Peary claimed to have covered more than 186 miles (300 km) in four days. This record speed has made some people doubt that Peary made it to the North Pole at all. Further, explorer Frederick A. Cook announced that he had already reached the North Pole a year earlier. Controversy surrounded this issue for decades. Although Peary's claim is more widely accepted than Cook's, there are serious doubts that either of the expeditions reached the North Pole.

FIRST TO THE POLES
PEARY AND AMUNDSEN REACH THE ENDS OF THE EARTH

NORWEGIAN EXPLORER Roald Amundsen wanted to be the first to reach the North Pole. When Peary *(opposite page)* claimed to be there first, Amundsen switched to the South Pole. His ship, the *Fram*, specially built for polar voyages, carried his expedition to the Bay of Whales. In October, 1911, he set out with four men, four sleds, and fifty-two dogs.

The first stage was across the Ross Ice Shelf. The expedition made progress across the flat ice, stopping for supplies already placed along part of the route by an advance party. Next came the climb up the rough ice of the Axel Heiberg **Glacier**. Terrible cold, gales, blizzards, hidden cracks in the ice, and other dangers loomed at all times. But Amundsen was confident. On December 14, the expedition successfully reached the South Pole and raised the Norwegian flag.

The Norwegians were not the only people in Antarctica that year. A British team, led by Captain Robert F. Scott, was also headed for the South Pole. On January 17, they reached the Pole but found the Norwegian flag already flying there. Tired and defeated, Scott's men turned back and perished on the journey.

Amundsen's journey to the South Pole was a well-planned expedition. Dogs pulled sleds loaded with supplies, while Amundsen's men traveled by their own power.

ANTARCTICA

South Pole

Ross Ice Shelf

SOUTHERN OCEAN

Amundsen's route 1911

The Norwegian Roald Amundsen (1872-1928) gave up his medical studies to be an explorer. Besides his polar conquest, he was the first to sail through the Northwest Passage in Arctic Canada.

41

THE HIGHEST POINT ON EARTH

EDMUND HILLARY AND TENZING NORGAY CLIMB MOUNT EVEREST

PEOPLE FIRST BEGAN CLIMBING mountains about two hundred years ago. But not until the twentieth century did anyone try to climb Mount Everest located on the border between Nepal and Tibet. It is the highest mountain in the world at 29,080 feet (8,863 m). Two British mountaineers, George Mallory and Andrew Irvine, *may* have reached the **summit** in 1924. They were last seen 820 feet (250 m) from the top before they disappeared. The Tibetans call Everest *Qomolangma,* "Mother Goddess of the World." Gales there blow at more than 93 miles (150 km) an hour.

In 1953, a British and Commonwealth expedition led by Colonel John Hunt set out to climb Mount Everest. Two men reached the South Summit but then had to turn back. Colonel Hunt chose two other climbers to make a second attempt. They were Edmund Hillary, a New Zealander, and Tenzing Norgay. Tenzing Norgay was a Sherpa, one of the native inhabitants of mountainous Nepal. The two men reached the top and stayed just fifteen minutes, worried about their oxygen supply. They made their way safely back down the mountain.

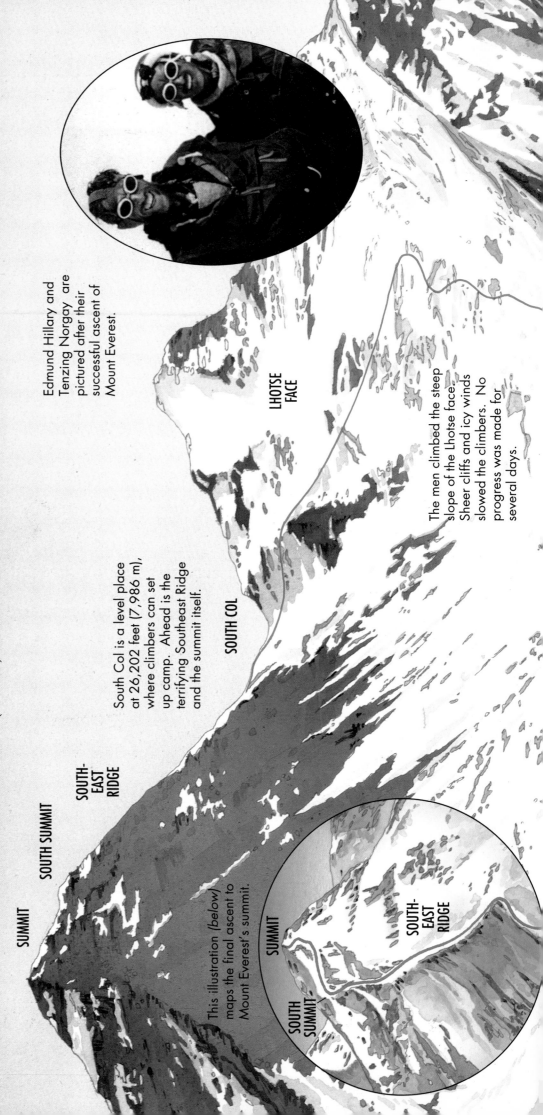

Edmund Hillary and Tenzing Norgay are pictured after their successful ascent of Mount Everest.

LHOTSE FACE

The men climbed the steep slope of the Lhotse face. Sheer cliffs and icy winds slowed the climbers. No progress was made for several days.

SOUTH COL

South Col is a level place at 26,202 feet (7,986 m), where climbers can set up camp. Ahead is the terrifying Southeast Ridge and the summit itself.

SOUTH-EAST RIDGE

SOUTH SUMMIT

SUMMIT

This illustration (*below*) maps the final ascent to Mount Everest's summit.

SOUTH SUMMIT

SUMMIT

SOUTH-EAST RIDGE

They climbed the sloping valley called Western Cwm. Several camps were established on the slopes. This route had been used only once before.

WESTERN CWM

KHUMBU ICEFALL

Base Camp was set up on the Khumbu Glacier at a height of 17,573 feet (5,356 m). It was a long, hard climb to reach this point. Ahead awaited the dangerous Khumbu Icefall.

KHUMBU GLACIER

CHINA

Tibet

Mt. Everest

NEPAL

INDIA

MYANMAR (BURMA)

PAKISTAN

NEARLY THERE!

On the Southeast Ridge, Edmund Hillary and Tenzing Norgay pitched camp. Hillary slept sitting up to stop the tent from blowing away. The next morning, the wind dropped, and the sun was bright. By 9 a.m., the men were on the South Summit. Ahead was a rock wall, 40 feet (12 m) straight up. They climbed it and stood on top of the world.

43

FIRST IN SPACE

FROM DREAMS TO REALITY

PEOPLE DREAMED of traveling in outer space long before rockets were invented. In 1865, the French science fiction writer Jules Verne wrote a story about travelers to the Moon. They arrived on the Moon in something that looked like a train!

The major factor that allowed space travel was the rocket, which needs no outside air to operate. It, therefore, can operate in the **vacuum** of outer space. The first person to suggest that rockets might be used for space flight was a Russian teacher, Konstantin Tsiolkovsky, in 1903. No one took much notice until American scientist Robert H. Goddard built the first successful rocket in 1926.

The Space Age really began on October 4, 1957, when the Soviet Union (now Russia) launched *Sputnik 1*, the first human-made satellite to **orbit** Earth. A dog named Laika was the first Earthly being to travel outside Earth's atmosphere, closely followed by the first human, Soviet **cosmonaut** Yuri Gagarin on April 12, 1961. His spacecraft, *Vostok 1*, made one orbit of Earth in a flight that lasted 108 minutes. The descent capsule, which measured just 7.5 feet (2.3 m) across, landed in Russia, but Gagarin was not in it. He had parachuted out at 22,000 feet (6,700 m).

THE FIRST SPACE WALK

Aleksei Leonov, an ex-fighter pilot from the Soviet Union (now Russia), trained as a cosmonaut. In 1965, he became the first person to walk in space when he exited his spacecraft, *Voskhod 2*. With the door to the spacecraft shut behind him, he entered outer space. Tied to the craft by a cable, Leonov spent ten minutes alone in space, filming the sights with a portable television camera.

In 1984, U.S. **astronaut** Captain Bruce McCandless became the first person to leave a spacecraft while in outer space and have no link to the spacecraft. He was the first human **satellite**. He and Colonel Bob Stewart were in outer space, outside their spacecraft, for five hours. They traveled in vehicles that looked like armchairs. The vehicles were fitted with gas-powered thrusters.

A YEAR IN SPACE

In the 1970s, the Soviets and the Americans began building space stations. Cosmonauts Musa Manarov and Vladimir Titov spent just short of 366 days in the Russian *Mir* space station in 1987-1988. Their record was broken by cosmonaut Valeri Poliakov in 1995. Poliakov still holds the record for longest distance traveled in space — about 250 million miles (402 million km). U.S. astronaut Shannon Lucid spent 188 days on board *Mir* in 1996. She was the first woman to be awarded the (U.S.) Congressional Space Medal of Honor.

The first woman in space was twenty-six-year-old cosmonaut Valentina Tereshkova *(right)*. She orbited Earth in *Vostok 6* 48 times in 1963.

Soviet Air Force Major Yuri Gagarin (1934-1968) *(right)*, a carpenter's son, made the first-ever piloted space flight in *Vostok 1* in 1961.

SPACE FIRSTS

October 4, 1957 Soviets launch *Sputnik 1*, first human-made satellite
April 12, 1961 Soviet cosmonaut Yuri Gagarin makes first flight in piloted spacecraft, *Vostok 1*
May 5, 1961 First U.S. astronaut Alan Shepard takes space flight
February 20, 1962 John Glenn becomes first U.S. astronaut to orbit Earth
June 16, 1963 Soviet cosmonaut Valentina Tereshkova becomes first woman in space
March 18, 1965 Soviet cosmonaut Aleksei Leonov makes first space walk
July 21, 1969 U.S. astronaut Neil Armstrong is the first person to walk on the Moon
February 7, 1984 U.S. astronaut Bruce McCandless makes first untethered space walk
1987-1988 Soviet cosmonauts Titov and Manarov spend a record 366 days in space

Neil Armstrong, *(right)* the first person to walk on the Moon

GLOSSARY

abdicated — officially gave up power.

aborigines — the native or original people of an area.

astronaut — a person from a country other than Russia who is trained for travel in outer space.

civilization — a group of people living in a certain part of the world that has developed language, art, science, and the means of making a living.

complex — a connected grouping of many items, such as buildings or stores.

cosmonaut — a person from Russia who is trained for travel in outer space.

cuneiform — made of or written in wedge-shaped characters.

gales — incredibly strong winds.

glacier — a mass of ice that forms from snow on mountaintops. It moves slowly down the mountain or through a valley.

hieroglyphs — ancient writings made with pictures.

legends — stories based on events that may have happened in history. The stories are handed down from generation to generation.

martial arts — sports that have their basis in combat.

merchants — people who buy and sell goods or who work in the trading or commerce industries.

minaret — a tower on top of a mosque where people gather to pray.

monarchy — a government or country that is ruled by a king or queen.

mutinied — rebelled against authority or the officers in charge.

nomads — people who move from place to place in order to find the necessary resources to survive.

obsidian — volcanic glass that is black in color.

orbit — to travel around an object in a circle.

pictograms — ancient or prehistoric drawings or paintings on rock walls.

prehistoric — belonging to the time before history was recorded, or written down.

satellite — an object in outer space that orbits another object in space.

shoguns — military governors that ruled Japan for centuries.

skyscraper — a tall building in a city that seems to "scrape" the sky.

summit — the highest point or peak; the top.

typhoons — strong tropical hurricanes.

vacuum — a space that contains no air.

RESEARCH PROJECTS

1. Make models to scale of the tallest structures in your area, such as office buildings or silos. How do these structures compare to the world's tallest buildings?

2. Create an alphabet using only pictures. With your pictograms, write messages and make lists. List your favorite musical groups, foods, movies, sports stars, and video games. See if your family and friends can translate your pictograms.

3. Research how many different types of bridges have existed. What is unique about each type that sets it apart from the other types?

4. Find out which countries have monarchies. How long have the monarchies existed? Did each one come about due to inheritance or by force?

5. What sports were in the first Olympics? How have the Olympic Games changed over the years? Have any new sports been added in recent years? What other sports would you like to see added to future Olympic Games?

BOOKS

Castles. Smith and Green (Watts)

Guinness Book of Olympic Records. (Facts on File)

Guinness Book of Records. (Facts on File)

How Skyscrapers Are Made. Michael (Facts on File)

Isaac Asimov's New Library of the Universe (series).
   Asimov (Gareth Stevens)

Isaac Asimov's Pioneers of Science and Exploration (series).
   Asimov (Gareth Stevens)

The Land of the Pharaohs. Terzi (Childrens Press)

Martial Arts. Reisberg (Watts)

Mountain Climbing. Hargrove and Johnson (Lerner)

Our Century (series). (Gareth Stevens)

Out of the Cradle: Exploring the Frontiers Beyond Earth.
   Hartmann (Workman)

Pictures of the Past (series). Allard (Gareth Stevens)

Sculpture. Widman (Prentice Hall)

Space Tour. Mackie (Hayes)

*Sputnik to Space Shuttle: The Complete Story of Space
   Flight.* Nicolson (Dodd, Mead)

The World Almanac. (World Almanac Books)

VIDEOS

Great Explorers. (National Geographic Society)

Himalayan Trekking: Sherpa Expeditions in Nepal.
   (Videotakes)

The Last Emperor. (Columbia)

The Mystery of the Pyramids. (Barr Films)

Olympics: The Eternal Torch. (AIMS Media)

Piloted Space Flights. (Gareth Stevens)

There Goes a Spaceship. (KidVision)

WEB SITES

www.seas.upenn.edu/%7Eahm/history.htm

www.ed.gov/pubs/parents/History/Home.html

www.nss.org/askastro

olympics.tufts.edu/

www.ernestallen.com/tr/CA/GuinnessWorldofRecords/

eawc.evansville.edu/index.htm

PLACES TO VISIT

The Space and Rocket Center and Space Camp
   One Tranquility Base
   Huntsville, AL 35807

Edmonton Space and Science Centre
   11211 - 142nd Street
   Edmonton, Alberta T5M 4A1

Museum of Science and Industry
   57th Street and Lake Shore Drive
   Chicago, IL 60637

Ontario Science Centre
   770 Don Mills Road
   Don Mills, Ontario M3C 1T3

Guinness World of Records Museum
   6767 Hollywood Boulevard
   Hollywood, CA 90028

Explorers Hall - National Geographic Society
   1145 17th Street NW
   Washington, D.C. 20036

INDEX